SIGNS & WONDERS

SIGNS & WONDERS

WHY PENTECOSTALISM IS THE WORLD'S FASTEST-GROWING FAITH

Paul Alexander

Foreword by
Martin E. Marty

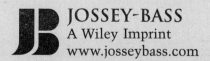
JOSSEY-BASS
A Wiley Imprint
www.josseybass.com

Published by Jossey-Bass
A Wiley Imprint
989 Market Street, San Francisco, CA 94103-1741—www.josseybass.com

Readers should be aware that Internet Web sites offered as citations and/or sources for further
information may have changed or disappeared between the time this was written and when it is read.

Limit of Liability/Disclaimer of Warranty: While the publisher and author have used their best
efforts in preparing this book, they make no representations or warranties with respect to the
accuracy or completeness of the contents of this book and specifically disclaim any implied
warranties of merchantability or fitness for a particular purpose. No warranty may be created or
extended by sales representatives or written sales materials. The advice and strategies contained
herein may not be suitable for your situation. You should consult with a professional where
appropriate. Neither the publisher nor author shall be liable for any loss of profit or any other
commercial damages, including but not limited to special, incidental, consequential, or other
damages.

Jossey-Bass books and products are available through most bookstores. To contact Jossey-Bass
directly call our Customer Care Department within the U.S. at 800-956-7739, outside the
U.S. at 317-572-3986, or fax 317-572-4002.

Credits appear on page 175.

Jossey-Bass also publishes its books in a variety of electronic formats. Some content that appears
in print may not be available in electronic books.

Library of Congress Cataloging-in-Publication Data:

Alexander, Paul, date.
  Signs & wonders : why Pentecostalism is the world's fastest-growing faith /
  Paul Alexander.—1st ed.
      p.   cm.
  Includes bibliographical references (p.   ) and index.
  ISBN 978-0-470-18396-0 (cloth)
  1. Pentecostalism.   I. Title.   II. Title: Signs and wonders.
    BR1644.A425 2009
    270.8'3—dc22
                                                                        2008053151

Printed in the United States of America
FIRST EDITION
HB *Printing*   10 9 8 7 6 5 4 3 2 1

CONTENTS

To all who allow the Spirit to guide
them into paths of peace.

FOREWORD

Since I am what many Pentecostals would call an "outsider" to their cultures and theologies, I have to introduce myself. For over fifty years I have been teaching and writing books and articles about Christianity (and sometimes other faiths). Most of the research and writing has dealt with North American Christianity, and includes some accounts of the rise and development of Pentecostalism and various charismatic movements. More recently my attention turned to a larger scene as I wrote a smallish book, *The Christian World: A Global History*. In the latter chapters of the book, as sub-Saharan Africa, Asia, and Latin America became the focus, Pentecostalism—though I had to treat it all too briefly—showed up as a face of the future of much of Christianity. One cannot deal fairly with twenty-first century Christian history without giving an ever-greater place to Pentecostalism.

Dazzled as I am by stories of Pentecostal growth and success, I remain outside the movement. Being the "other" at many kinds of Christian gatherings is not a new situation. There are 38,000 Christian denominations at latest account, but every few minutes that number changes. While many of these denominations represent families of churches or are parts of coalitions, councils, or partnerships, the number of Christian phenomena remains almost incomprehensibly huge. When I attended and reported on the Second Vatican Council, though I share the basic faith and the creeds and stories, I was a "non-Catholic" presence. In the Eastern world, the Orthodox think of me as "the other," and, vice versa I have to add. When I am part of a convention or congress self-labeled "Evangelical," I get introduced as "this year's non-Evangelical representative." I respond by noting that ordinarily I am the only person in the room who belongs to a church body with the word "Evangelical" in it—the Evangelical Lutheran Church in America.

That may be more autobiography than you need or want, but I hope those paragraphs help set the stage for what follows, and can serve as a kind of invitation to an audience that does not share all the presuppositions of the actors on stage. Similarly, I hope that those readers who are Pentecostal will remember that their word and world and workings need translation— which is what Paul Alexander's book offers—if that audience is to make some sense of Pentecostalism. My guide in these matters is the philosopher Spinoza, who wrote that when he set out to understand complex phenomena, he made a sedulous effort not to laugh, not to cry, not to denounce, not to judge, but to understand. In that spirit I have read much Pentecostal literature, met with Pentecostal scholars, attended gatherings, always sympathetically, but never to the point that I am led to shared convictions.

Perhaps some winced when I described myself as an "outsider." The Pentecostal reach, scope, and mission is generous and expansive, and in many ways it may not want to condemn anyone to outsiderhood or the status of the stranger. One can almost hear a hearty "y'all come!" from Pentecostals and a quiet narrative base invitation from Professor Alexander. What I meant by stressing the "stranger" status is to remind readers of the hermeneutical situation. By hermeneutics here is meant an endeavor to understand a phenomenon—and Pentecostalism is certainly a phenomenon!—by observing carefully, parking one's presuppositions at the door insofar as that is possible—and by being aware of how such differing presuppositions color what is said and done.

To take an illustration of ecumenical importance. Christians believe in baptism—I am speaking of what Pentecostals would call "the first baptism," with a second one to follow—but they bring different interpretations of the biblical narratives, commands, and promises. Give all the biblical texts that allude to baptism to a Christian from an infant-baptizing community on one hand and the same text to one who believes that only older children and adults should be baptized by immersion. Give the same text to believers in "Catholic" and "mainline" Protestant traditions who baptize in various forms, though always with water. Have some of each attend the same seminary, the same conferences, the same gatherings, and let them then converse. A year goes by, and then a lifetime. Some from either camp may convert to the other, and all will profit from joint study. But assumptions that participants bring color what they find and how they interpret it. It is not that only one set is prejudiced and the other not. Nor, let me hasten to add, is there seldom movement from one camp to another, though conversions do occur; how else could Pentecostal movements gain new millions, not all of them babies!

It is urgent that Christians everywhere work (and are graced) to understand "the other." In their various bodies they make up one-third of the population of the world, and pray and engage in mission to gain more to the fold. If they are ignorant of each other, mistrustful of others, unwilling to keep each other in prayer, grieve at the losses of others, or fail to celebrate the joys and victories of others, they harm the Christian cause and stand in the way of the movement of the spirit. Does this spirit of understanding and welcome undercut the efforts to clarify and expound the faith? Do friendly reaches across boundaries mean that conviction has to be lessened, and that everything has to turn soft and mushy? Not at all. Whoever confesses participation in the Body of Christ, and who celebrates "one Lord, one faith, one baptism, one God and Father of us all" can turn his or her back on others or fail to accept the gift and share the tasks with others, misses out on so much and thwarts the movement of the spirit.

A committed Lutheran, I am also a committed ecumenist. Some would say that it is important to draw boundaries. We all know, tragically, that there are boundaries between and among Pentecostals and non-Pentecostals. These can become barriers on both and all sides of these sects, and schisms, spite, and even hatred can rule. Asked why I am curious about Pentecostalism, am awed by its appeal (especially in the "poor world," where growth is so impressive), and beguiled by the diversity it represents, I answer, "for the same reason I am interested and hope to feel welcome in the circles of Eastern Orthodox Christianity and other parts of the church which are not my natural home."

So I urge the reading of Paul Alexander's *Signs and Wonders* as a second-best introduction to Pentecostalism, the first being "being there." He offers a clear narrative line, issues helpful explanations, and gives something of the experience one recognizes at Pentecostal events or in Pentecostal ventures. While I have studied the Pentecostal experience as it has been analyzed by biblical scholars, theologians, philosophers, historians, psychologists, anthropologists, phenomenologists, and liturgiologists—what a cluster of scholarly "sects" we have engendered and enjoyed—most of them keep the reader or observer at a distance. They tend to be "objective" and "reductionist," meaning that they "reduce" what they are studying to something else. (So Pentecostalism is reduced to something being explicable as a movement of the poor or, formerly, the uneducated, or the psychologically needy.) Alexander is not "objective," though he is fair-minded, and he is not a "reductionist," because he takes Pentecostalism seriously on its members' own terms. That is why one may learn, or why I learned, much from it.

Not that I left my analytical hat and skeptical spectacles in the next room as I read. "Try the spirits!" is a biblical command and an injunction to historians, who are not to be gullible, nor to accept every conflicting thing because somebody utters it or claims it. So I have to say that I winced in some stories, winked when some explanations asked too much of me, kept my fingers crossed as I turned pages—and yet was strangely moved and, again, figuratively taken by the hand and walked through Pentecostalism in the Bible, in Christian history, around the globe. The book is simple but not simplistic, moving as it does between technical subjects made comprehensible and obvious topics rendered subtly.

In a couple of cases the author talks about Pentecostal swindles or scandals; there have been enough of these to embarrass the movement. Still, when hundreds of millions of Christians are part of it, one has to expect some shocks. Think of the Catholic-clergy sexual scandals, also a blight on a part of the church which numbers a billion faithful and semi-faithful. In a couple of cases he seems unconvinced of the authenticity when something drastically beyond the norm occurs, as in the case of some healing. Yet at other times he reports sympathetically and shows that he regards a phenomenon as valid and compelling. He is especially good at accounting for Pentecostal surges and successes. I might have liked some more attention to the works of mercy, and sometimes of justice, which characterize Pentecostal congregational and individual lives in many places. Maybe they'll receive their due in a Volume II.

For those of us who keep our guard up as we hear extravagant claims, it is valuable to read someone who drops his guard. In the nineteenth century it was said of a skeptical modernist theologian that it is frustrating to be told in advance what to believe. Alexander does not frustrate, and allows the believers to speak for themselves as they witness to and manifest what will strike fair-minded "other" Christians as signs of the Spirit.

Martin E. Marty

Martin E. Marty is the Fairfax M. Cone Distinguished Service Professor Emeritus at the University of Chicago and an ordained Lutheran minister.

ACKNOWLEDGMENTS

This book was not my idea, and sometimes it takes someone else to see the possibility of a book in you that you never knew you had. Sheryl Fullerton has that gift, and I will be forever grateful. Sheryl is an amazing executive editor at Jossey-Bass who said no to me when I pitched a book about Pentecostals, peacemaking, and social justice and in the same breath asked, "But why is Pentecostalism such a fast-growing faith?" I offered her a few thoughts, and she said, "Write a book about that." Thank you, Sheryl.

I never could have written this book if I didn't have the heritage of being raised in the vibrant (and sometimes odd) Pentecostal faith. So I gladly acknowledge all the folks in the Sedan Assembly of God in Sedan, Kansas, where I spent thousands of church services growing up, and Wheat State Camp where I went every summer. The churches, college, and seminary I attended shaped me into a born and bred Pentecostal. Even though I rejected Pentecostalism and distanced myself from it during my twenties, I am thankful for the inspiring and empowering aspects of this global movement that the process of writing this book helped me discover anew.

I am also deeply indebted to people at Azusa Pacific University for the flexibility and schedule they provided for me so that I could write, and I especially appreciate the conversations with my colleagues that strengthened this book. Special thanks to Arlene Sanchez-Walsh and Don Thorsen for particularly helpful insights.

Many friends also dialogued with me and shared wonderful stories and ideas from their own experiences: Jonathan and Brenda Jeter, Don and Carissa Niemyer, Jarred and Kathy Stover, Chris and Erica Ramirez, Brian and Shannon Pipkin, Nick and Kimbra Stuva, Carol Vasquez, and other friends who requested that I not divulge their names.

My family helped me before I ever started writing and then offered advice, memories, critiques, and inspiration all the way through the process. I so thoroughly appreciate the love and prayers of Grandma and Grandpa Alexander, Grandma and Grandpa Smith, Grandma and Grandpa Bird, Grandma Velma, Mom, Dad, Mark, Joy, Breleigh, Judah, Levi, Rodney, Betty, Ronda, Rick, Teri, Jason, Jorilyn, and Raegan. I'm glad we're family.

The highlight of my writing days at home was having my children occasionally peek around the door of my office-bedroom with a grin and announce, "Only two more hours and you have to quit working." And without fail they would show up at 5:00 P.M. on the dot to pull me into the backyard to play tag or into the living room in hopes of some video game time. We tried not to miss any bike rides, library Saturdays, or games of baseball or Dinotopia to get this book done, but sometimes a trip home from Sea World included me pulling out the laptop in the car and finishing up a chapter while Deborah drove and Nathan and Kharese read. So I want to say a humongous thank-you to my children for bringing me sandwiches, drawing pictures for me to sticky-tack around my desk, and never ever letting me forget that they are much more important than this book.

Finally, I happily acknowledge the patience, encouragement, and stimulating insights of my wife and muse, Deborah. Whenever I would read a passage to her, she'd spout off some witty remark that often sparked a new idea, and she graciously helped create space for me to reflect. This book would not be possible without her. Thanks.

SIGNS &
WONDERS

CHAPTER 1

JUST ASK: A WORLD OF MIRACLES AWAITS

Expect a new miracle every day.

—*Oral Roberts*

When I was a kid, growing up on a farm in Kansas, my younger brother, Mark, and I loved to swim in our pond out in the pasture. We would jump and dive off the dock into the deep, cold water, swim back, and climb up the old aluminum ladder that we had stuck in the mud and leaned against the rickety pier. We had truck and tractor inner tubes we floated on and a canoe we would paddle around in.

When I turned twelve, I think it was, I got a new waterproof digital watch for my birthday. One hot summer afternoon not long after that, Mark pushed an inner tube out away from the dock for me to dive through. As I dived through the tube, the valve stem caught my watch and ripped it off my wrist. My heart sank; I swam back to the dock and told Mark what had happened. I then started diving to the bottom of the pond, which was more than eight feet deep at the end of the dock, running my hands through the mud, trying to find that watch.

After diving several times with no luck, I was exhausted, frustrated, and ready to give up and go back to the house. Mark, being a good little Pentecostal boy, suggested that we pray. I didn't feel like it, but being a good Pentecostal big brother, I agreed. Mark prayed a very simple prayer: "Dear God, please help us find Paul's watch. In the name of Jesus, amen." He raised up his little head and looked me right in the face, grinning, with his eyes sparkling as if it were Christmas morning. He suggested that he swim back out with the inner tube and put it in the exact same spot for me to dive through again. Doubting that this would work or that we'd ever find the watch, I nevertheless directed him from the dock—a bit farther out, a bit to the right—until he had placed the inner tube perfectly. I backed up, ran down the dock, dived through the inner tube, and then swam to the bottom of the pond with my eyes squeezed shut and my hands spread wide open until they hit the cold squishy mud. My right palm landed directly on my watch; I didn't even have to move my hand around to find it. I grasped it tightly and swam back to the surface, hardly believing what had just happened. Mark and I ran back to the house and talked all over each other telling our mom.

That story has become a little legend in our family. But legend though it may be, it's not an odd or unbelievable event in the lives of Pentecostals. Like Mark, most Pentecostals expect things like this to happen and love to tell stories about the miracles and healings. Just this past Christmas, I told the tale of my lost-and-found watch to my in-laws in Texas while we were all sitting around the dinner table eating stew and cornbread. Ronda, my sister-in-law, immediately said, "Remember the bone spur on my knee that disappeared?" and Betty, my mother-in-law, interjected, "And don't forget the burns on Deborah's leg that were healed." Grandma then told about the time that Grandpa laid his hands on their van and prayed for it one morning—which was the morning they were almost killed by an out-of-control eighteen-wheeler "with smoke boiling everywhere" that "screeched within two feet of the back of our van." When asked why he had prayed that morning, Grandpa replied, "I just felt impressed to do it. Never done it before and never done it since." Betty then told us about when her uncle had a spider bite so bad that he swelled up and was going to die. There was no doctor, so his father prayed for the boy, who was healed immediately.

Everybody chimed in with one story after another until Grandpa interrupted, "I'm going to tell one even more impressive than that," and went on to recount an amazing tale about when Sister Foster had called him to come quickly because Gladys, with the death rattle in her throat, had been sent home to die by the doctors. Her husband, whom Grandpa called "a big ol' Methodist," was standing by the door "to see what we were going to do to his wife." Grandma and Grandpa prayed for her, and a couple of days later, she was perfectly fine and lived for many years after that.

Grandpa then told about how, when he was stricken with appendicitis as a twelve-year-old boy, he looked at a clock on the wall and thought, "The man who made that clock could fix it if it broke. And God could fix me, too." The pain left him that very instant, and he just swung his feet off the bed and got up and strolled out onto the porch. His father walked up from fetching the doctor, leaned against a post, and, said Grandpa, "his eyes got yay big, and he said, 'Son, what's happened to you?' I told him about the clock and how the pain left me. He expected me to get sicker and sicker; he just knew I was going to die. But I was playing with the other boys from then on, and I've never had another pain on that side."

Over the next hour, almost everyone at the table told at least one story. We heard tales of healings and miracles that included asthma cured, a cancer that fell off a man's hand, infected tonsils being spit out on the ground by a boy after he was prayed for, and the woman whose infected bladder healed ("She still writes to us fifty-five years later," Grandma said with a nod of her head). There was the woman in Anniston, Alabama, who had emphysema; Brother Cobb in Bonham, Texas, who also had emphysema (and who slept in a bed for the first time in fifteen years after being prayed for and healed); the woman with unceasing pain that had lasted for years (who heard a radio preacher say, "Go to the nearest Assembly of God church and get the pastor to pray for you"); the two-year-old girl who didn't pray quite right ("Thank you Jesus *for* mommy's headache") but her mother's headache was healed anyway; and even a healing from "we don't know what it was."

During a pause in our merry recounting of miracle upon miracle, I mentioned that in my book I would also need to address the fact that sometimes people aren't healed, that sometimes miracles don't happen when we pray. At my words, silence fell; I could hear the clock ticking in the living room. I took a bite of my stew, put some butter on another piece of cornbread, and drank some sweet tea. Then Grandpa broke the silence by telling about the man who had "walking pneumonia" and couldn't eat onions, but after Grandpa prayed for him, he ate steak sautéed with onions and was fine from then on. Betty told about how Rodney, her husband, who was a technician at an Exxon gas plant, was healed of plantar warts and his feet ended up as smooth as a baby's bottom. There followed more stories—about how prayer healed the boy who sucked down a peanut whole, shell and all, and doctors thought he'd die; the boy who was sweating with a terrible fever in bed (probably from polio) and was perfectly well the next day; and the junior high girls who made it safely home from basketball practice in the middle of a tornado-filled hailstorm: "Suddenly there was a clearing around them. They drove home safely with the storm all around, but their car area was clear. They got inside safely. It built the girls' faith incredibly." Those girls personally experienced a miracle like all the ones we'd been recounting, and in the future, when the need arose, they'd be able to have even more confidence when they prayed.

When I told the story about finding my watch, I did not expect that it would generate a slew of miracle stories. But I should have, because the four generations of people sitting around that table really believe these things happen—and happen regularly if we pray with enough faith that God can do them. Not only have they heard hundreds of stories like these, but they've seen some of them first hand. And the silent response to my question about the lack of healings is as revealing as the healing stories themselves: Pentecostals tend not to tell about the times their prayers go unanswered and miracles don't happen. They often do just what Grandpa did—fill the silence with more inspiring miracle stories.

My little experience that winter afternoon is not unique; more than half a billion other Pentecostals in the world expect the same kind of amazing miracles when they ask God to help them. They live in a world where God is close enough to talk to, friendly enough to care about warts, and powerful enough to keep an eighteen-wheeler from crushing your van.

It is not my intention here to defend or prove that these stories and events are true. The people who experience these miracles believe that they happen. I know there are many questions about a God who does things like this, and I know that many other explanations can be given as to why these things happened (if they happened at all). For instance, if God can heal, why would God not just heal everybody, or at least a lot more people? It makes no sense to heal a few children miraculously but let thousands of others die. Or perhaps the healings are not by God but are the results of wish fulfillment or the placebo effect. Some theorists have even suggested that humans have the ability to release energy that can heal themselves and even others sometimes, but it's not God's doing; it's just a phenomenon that's not yet understood. But in the Pentecostal world, healings and miracles are normal, everyday events, and they're attributed to God. Pentecostals look at it this way: if it happens sometimes, why question it? Keep praying and believing, and your miracle may come.

Jesus and His Followers Healed People— It's in the Bible!

So where do Pentecostals get the idea that God responds in miraculous ways when people pray? The answer is simple: it's in the Bible. It tells of more than forty miracles and healings that Jesus did, and one biblical author even had the audacity to add that "the whole world could not contain the books if all his works were written down in detail."[1] Jesus restored a blind man's sight, raised a dead little girl back to life, calmed a storm while in a boat on a lake, straightened crippled limbs, cured skin diseases, and turned water into wine. People like Pentecostals, who read the Bible in a straightforward way and take it as gospel, are impressed by these miracles and healings. But what of those who object that just because Jesus worked miracles, does that mean that people today should think they could do the same? Pentecostalism has a response for them.

Pentecostals believe that Jesus was telling the truth when he said, "I assure you that if anyone believes in me, they will be able to do the same things that I do; and they will do even greater things than these, because I am going back to the Father."[2] They believe that after Jesus came back to life following his execution, he empowered all of his followers to pray, heal, and trust God for miracles, just as Jesus himself had done. In fact, the amazing stories start immediately after Pentecost—that's the day Jesus filled his friends with the Holy Spirit so they could live like him and tell people about him and help them live as Jesus did. Peter healed a crippled man on the steps of the temple within a month of Jesus' being gone, others "performed many miraculous signs and wonders among the people," and Paul raised a dead boy back to life. James wrote that "if you are sick, ask the mature believers to come and pray for you. Ask them to put olive oil on you in the name of the Lord. Prayers offered in faith will make sick people well. The Lord will heal them, and if they have sinned, he will forgive them."[3] These are not just a few random stories and instructions thrown together to make a case; Pentecostals believe that the miraculous was a regular and expected part of what God was doing through his people in the early years of Christianity and that God still wants Christians to live this same way.

Pentecostals have been severely criticized since the beginning of the movement for believing in modern-day healings and miracles. Some Christians argue that miracles were just for the first century, the first few generations of Christianity, the Bible days. They say that such things died out hundreds of years ago and that God doesn't work that way anymore. But Pentecostals believe they have both the Bible and experience on their side; how else could they keep doing what others say can't be done? They really believe that everything that happened in the Bible can happen now, that all Christians everywhere in the world are supposed to be a continuation of the Bible days and can look to God for miracles. If asked, a Pentecostal would say that right now anyone, including you, can ask God to heal you . . . and it might just happen.

Praying with Faith: How It Works

Pentecostals have many ways of reasoning about how praying with faith works. I've heard that "faith is stepping out on nothing and landing on something." Like the little boy in *The Polar Express* who had to believe *before* he could see Santa Claus, Pentecostals trust that they're going to be OK even when all the evidence appears to weigh against them. You have to *believe* that it is possible. The Gospel according to Mark reports that Jesus said, "And these signs will accompany those who believe, in my name they will . . . place their hands on sick people and they will get well."[4] Only by truly believing can miraculous things happen; it's kind of like working with God, receiving what God really wants for us. Believing is agreeing with God. The Assemblies of God (with over forty million members worldwide) says it this way: "We take these Scriptures at face value and openly practice them in our church. We don't claim to be successful 100 percent of the time, but we persist in asking God to show his love and concern in tangible ways when the human body is suffering. And he does."[5] Pentecostals also place great significance on Jesus' saying that "in my name" miracles will happen. They pray "in the name of Jesus" and believe it is the most powerful name in the world, claiming that prayers prayed specifically in the name of Jesus are much more effective than any other prayers.

Some Pentecostal theologians and pastors have critiqued the stereotypical "name it and claim it" and "blab it and grab it" approach to healings and miracles. These are pejorative references to the teaching that Christians can simply name and claim the objects of their desire—physical healing, a new car, a watch at the bottom of the pond—and if they have enough faith, they will receive them. Detractors say that these kinds of Pentecostals just seem to be blabbing with their mouth and grabbing with their hands. They argue that the miraculous most often happens on the boundary between believers and unbelievers, because healings are supposed to be signs that God is real and the gospel is true. Miracles are evidence for the outsider, not therapy or a lottery for the insider. But even in the right context, the people praying are supposed to believe that God can heal; some even say you're supposed to believe that God will do the healing right then and there. Pentecostals tend to emphasize the human side of the equation, since God's ability is rarely questioned.

The witness of Pentecostals all around the world to miraculous events is understood to enhance people's ability to believe. When Fidel Castro reportedly sent a spy to investigate an underground Pentecostal church in Cuba, the pastor was preaching on healing, and many people were being healed. In the story, the spy arrived with a rotten and infected tooth and left with a new tooth and no pain. The church was never bothered again. Daniel Ekechukwu, a pastor in Nigeria who was supposedly killed in a car wreck and taken to the mortuary, where he lay for two days, was allegedly raised from the dead in 2001. The video chronicling the miracle includes interviews with the doctor and the mortician.[6] One of the reasons Pentecostals tell stories of miraculous events is that they know that healing works better and people have more faith when they see or hear about other things that God has done.

Faith also works better when it is exercised often and by as many people as possible. Pentecostals pray for healings and miracles for themselves and for others all the time. Prayer is certainly not limited to Sunday morning church services or to prayers by the pastor. There are prayer chains, prayer Web sites and e-mail lists, altar calls, spontaneous prayers, prayers on the phone, prayer requests, and "anointing with oil."

Prayer chains are networks of people who agree to call others when they receive a request or hear of an emergency. Before the days of e-mail and text messaging, the first person would telephone five people, and each of them would call five, who would call five, so that as many as fifty-six people could be praying about a problem within thirty minutes. When my mom got a call, we started praying while she made the rest of the calls. She kept the conversations short so she could move on down her list quickly, because the more people "bombarding heaven's gates," the greater the chances that the answer would come.

Spontaneous prayers may happen during the middle of a conversation anywhere—on a sidewalk or in a restaurant or any other place—if the person you're talking to suggests praying for something you're talking about. As for anointing oil, the use and type varies widely, but many Pentecostals take any ordinary cooking oil and gently dab it first on their fingers and then on the forehead of the person they're praying for. I've even heard about a man who used motor oil in an emergency because he didn't have his regular anointing oil. Praying with faith in the name of Jesus, believing thoroughly and without doubt that God can heal, and anointing with oil—these all work together to help produce the needed miracle.

But Does It Make Sense?

Our son was born a week late and weighed almost nine pounds. We were thrilled and excited, and so was our entire family. My parents (Pentecostals from Kansas), my wife Deborah's parents

(Pentecostals from Texas), grandparents, siblings, nieces, and cousins (all Pentecostals) crowded into the hospital room for the announcement of his name: Nathan Bird Alexander, after my middle name and Deborah's maiden name. Everyone was smiling and laughing, some even crying with joy, and celebrating. We had been married almost seven years, we had already been through one miscarriage, and everybody was eager for us to have a baby!

But a couple of hours later, Nathan began breathing much too rapidly; he was admitted immediately to the special care unit. He had some kind of serious virus or infection; we could not snuggle or sleep with him at all that first night, since he was under an oxygen dome. Deborah's blood pressure went way up because she was not holding her baby or able to nurse, and by the second day, we were aware that he might not recover. Of course, our family was praying for Nathan, but I was not. I couldn't.

I had recently finished my coursework for a Ph.D. in theology, and that can be a painful and disconcerting experience for a Pentecostal. I had also become more aware of the depth of suffering in the world, and much of the Christianity I had grown up with made little or no sense to me anymore. How, I wondered, could I ask God to heal my son when hundreds of thousands, even millions of children around the world were starving, abused, suffering with disease, and dying every day? It was not fair. If God cared for this world half as much as my wife does or loved this world as much as the Bible says he does, he wouldn't make us jump through hoops of faith-filled, word-specific "in the name of Jesus" prayer in order for him to heal people. The whole world needs healing. I want it to be healed and would do so, if I had the power, without making anyone ask in just the right way. Isn't God also that kind? That merciful? That gracious? That realistic?

I had concluded that the completely messed-up nature of the world could not be reconciled with the existence of an all-powerful and all-loving God. If God is all-powerful (he can do anything), then he *can* heal; if he is all-loving (he wants the best for everybody), he *will* heal; yet all are *not* healed. Therefore, I reasoned, God is either not all-powerful or not all-loving, or there is no God. A powerful but unloving God would not mind that so many people in the world are suffering—I couldn't buy that. A loving God without so much power is more believable given the fact that the world is in such bad shape. God cares immensely but can't fix everything.

So as a Pentecostal who had struggled immensely with the reality of pain in the world (even though not so much in my personal life), at this moment of great need in my family I could no longer pray for healing. For if God can heal and do miracles but does so only based on human prayers, I felt I could no longer respect or worship such an arbitrary and finicky being; a loving God would not play games with people who are in the depths of despair and suffering. I had quit believing that God heals at all. It was either that or return to atheism.

Pentecostals have answers to questions and frustrations like mine. "Trust in God's wisdom," they say, or "You need to have more faith," or "It's not God's timing." Each of these answers helps Pentecostals make sense of their world.

But telling a woman with multiple sclerosis that she would be healed if she would get the sin out of her life could very well drive her away (as it did a friend of mine). Another friend, raised Pentecostal, had severe arthritis that kept him in a wheelchair most of the time. He eventually had to leave Pentecostalism because he got tired of being told he needed more faith in order to be healed.

The problem with believing in miracles and healings is that they don't always happen—and when they don't happen, somebody gets blamed. Because healing is seen as a certainty for those with enough faith, it seems there has to be an explanation when prayers don't heal the sick. I blamed God for not just healing everybody, but most Pentecostals won't do that. They trust God and instead often find fault in their own prayers or in the lives of the people who are not healed. Pentecostals are told to work up their faith like they are building their muscles.

But this sometimes sounds like faith in faith, not faith in God. The responsibility falls so heavily on the prayers and faith of the people that failure is taken very personally. After all, Pentecostals believe unquestioningly in God's ability to heal. So if it doesn't happen, it's not God's fault; God can choose not to heal, but many think that if he does not heal, it's because he wasn't asked properly. We can cause God's hand to move if we believe hard enough and say the right words ("in the name of Jesus").

In a way, I've come to think that this kind of Pentecostalism is like a Harry Potter or *Lord of the Rings* type of Christianity. You live in a world where there are demons, spirits, and miraculous happenings within your control. And like the phenomenal global success of the Harry Potter series (with hundreds of millions of copies sold so far), Pentecostalism has drawn millions of followers.

The reason for the appeal of Pentecostalism may lie in the natural, simple human desire to have more control and power over our lives and circumstances. Throughout history we have sought to improve our lives through knowledge, science, education, violence, medicine, religion, and magic. It is exciting to learn about something new that can help us improve ourselves, whether it is a better water pump in Kenya, an antidote for AIDS, a bigger bomb, or a more effective way to pray. Pentecostals believe that all humans can learn how to trust God for miracles, cast out demons, and heal the sick. Many even believe that people can be transported from one place to another instantly. When I was a teenager, I prayed for this to happen to me while driving late one night, exhausted. I didn't want to get into a wreck, and I had heard stories of such transportation happening—people were about out of gas and then suddenly they were fifty miles up the road—so I asked God for it to happen to me. It didn't, but I still believed it was possible, and I made it safely home anyway. (By the way, miraculous transportation happens several times in the Bible,[7] and it's a normal way of moving around for Harry Potter and his friends.)

When Harry Potter discovered that he was a wizard, not just a Muggle (a nonmagical person), he began a journey of empowerment that enabled him to make the world a better place. He learned how to cast spells and change his environment; things were different because he knew magic. Becoming a Pentecostal is like finding out that you're really a wizard; you really can change the world with supernatural power. And here's the kicker: weird things actually do happen in the real world. Everybody has a worldview by which they explain odd, unnatural, "miraculous" events. The Pentecostal worldview just puts a lot of trust in the unseen and the human ability to ask God for miracles. It's a way of life that sometimes yields remarkable results.

When fervent prayers don't yield the expected results, Pentecostals trust in "God's timing." This approach empowers Pentecostals to pray for the same thing year after year, even when what they pray for doesn't happen. There are many stories about the patience and perseverance of the praying mother who, after decades of prayer, finally saw her miracle. Jesus even tells a story about a persistent widow who keeps bothering a judge with her request for justice "to show his disciples that they should always pray and not give up."[8]

My seasons of unbelief or doubt, like the one I was in when my son was born, don't seem to sway many Pentecostals. They feel sorry for me and wish I believed; they pray for me and trust that I will come back to Pentecostal faith. They disagree with me and see my doubt as hurtful and sad, especially if I won't pray for healing when it is needed. When my newborn son was so ill, they prayed for him when I couldn't, and five days after he was born, we brought him home. And as a new father standing over his crib watching him sleep, counting his breaths to make sure they weren't too fast, I wished that I could pray for him. I really did. But his recovery had not helped me recover my faith; I could explain his health in many other ways. He received good medical care; we found out that he didn't have the worst-feared virus—I did not believe that God had healed him. My son was fine, and I was more relieved than I could ever put into words, but there were still millions of others suffering around the world, and it still wasn't fair, especially if Nathan was healed because God did it in answer to a few people's fervent prayers. I both did and didn't want there to be a God who heals and does miracles; I couldn't make it make sense.

While I was writing that last paragraph, I got a call from my mother in Kansas. She said, "I need you to help me pray for Dad's safety. He's on his way to Grandma's in the ice and snow with chains on his tires. Pray for Grandma; she just got bit by her cat and it's pretty bad. And pray for all of us, your uncle and aunts too, because she got bit two weeks ago and didn't tell the doctor or any of the rest of us. Help me pray for those three things." That was all. She told me she loved me, said good-bye, and hung up. She had called me to pray to change the world, to actually alter the future, to bring about a different reality because we are talking to the living God who cares about my Dad driving seven miles on roads covered in two inches of solid ice in the dead of winter. She expects him to be safer, Grandma to heal quicker, and the family to deal with this better because I am praying with her. So I did. It's been nine years since my son recovered, and the miraculous still doesn't make rational sense to me. The Bible tells about a sick boy's father who once said to Jesus, "I do believe. Help my unbelief."[9] I believe, and I don't believe, and I prayed with my mom anyway.

What's the Appeal?

I think there are four simple reasons that the Pentecostal approach to healings and miracles appeals to hundreds of millions of people around the world: almost everyone experiences difficulties, almost everyone needs hope, healing stories are in the Bible, and healing stories abound in contemporary life.

First, almost everybody in the world has at least one problem they'd like to have solved or fixed, whether it is physical, emotional, financial, relational, or occupational. We get sick, we get depressed, we need money, we fight with our spouses, and our coworkers annoy us. Pentecostalism creates a place where these problems can be presented to God immediately and continually; Pentecostals will pray with you about any problem whatsoever. And if it's physical healing you need, they'll sometimes ask you right after they're done praying, "Do you feel better?" Please don't let my down-home country personal stories mislead you—most Pentecostals, just like most of the rest of the earth's human inhabitants, live in cities. Over the past century, urban dwellers have increased from 14 percent of the world's population to over 50 percent. City people have at least as many problems as their rural cousins. And people who are hurting, even if they're urbanites, can be pleasantly surprised when someone offers to pray for their problem.

The second reason this appeals to so many people is that believing in healing and the miraculous is hopeful. It might actually happen, and as many Pentecostals say, "You'll never know if you don't pray." Poets, philosophers, and world-changers have reflected eloquently on how essential hope is to human survival. Martin Luther King Jr. said, "If you lose hope, somehow you lose the vitality that keeps life moving, you lose that courage to be, that quality that helps you go on in spite of it all."[10] When I was in the Middle East, I heard both Israelis and Palestinians encouraging themselves and others to "keep hope alive."

In difficult times, we need a reason to hope. And many Pentecostals think there is good scientific evidence to back up their experience and hope that prayers for healing work. Books like *The Faith Factor: Proof of the Healing Power of Prayer*, coauthored by Dale Matthews, a Yale-, Duke-, and Princeton-educated physician who teaches at Georgetown University, certainly help their case.[11] Such books—there are hundreds of them (some more theological than scientific)—argue that prayer has been proved to do such things as send cancer into remission and reverse heart disease. Even while my theological questioning caused me to quit believing that God healed, and even during my stint as a convinced atheist, I still had to admit that such things as these miraculous healings did occur. I considered them in terms of quantum physics or human energy, something explicable by science, rather than thinking that God in the classical Christian sense played a part, but I regained a hope that healings were real and possible.

So even though there will be differences of opinions among people regarding why these miraculous things happen, Pentecostals have a ready-made worldview that explains the seemingly unexplainable and provides very real hope in apparently impossible situations. In response to a question like "What am I supposed to do, just hope for a miracle?" the answer is "No, you and I are supposed to pray for one and believe that it could happen, because it can."

The third reason the Pentecostal perspective attracts so many people is that healings happened in the Bible. Quoting the most printed and best-selling book of all time and referencing Jesus himself is a pretty convincing argument for a whole lot of people in the world. The Qur'an also teaches that Jesus healed people, walked on water, and raised the dead. When my wife and I were on our honeymoon in Colorado, we had a Muslim taxi driver, and as a good Pentecostal, I felt I should tell him about Jesus. So thinking that I would get his attention and draw him to Christ, I said, "Do you believe in healing?" He told me that his father was healed of blindness when an imam (a Muslim religious leader) prayed for him. He witnessed to me!

Most religions value holy books, and spirituality is alive and well around the world. Most people believe in the one God, a pantheon of gods, or some kind of spirit or higher power. Pentecostalism affirms that belief in the divine and miraculous and specializes in it. Pentecostals are the ones who take the healing teachings in the Bible seriously and put them into practice, regardless of whether they are African, Asian, or American. There's an old saying: "The Bible says it, I believe it, and that settles it." That unassailable belief in the Bible may explain some of the appeal.

Finally, there is an almost infinite multitude of stories and personal experiences of people who have been healed or have witnessed a miracle. There is safety, and persuasion, in numbers. If accounts of Jesus' works in the New Testament have sold millions of copies, can you imagine how many planets it would take to hold the stories of the accomplishments of his millions of followers? A ten-country survey (of Brazil, Chile, Guatemala, Nigeria, Kenya, South Africa, India, the Philippines, South Korea, and the United States) conducted in 2006 found that large majorities of Pentecostals, from 56 percent in South Korea to 87 percent in Kenya, have personally experienced or witnessed the healing of an illness or injury.[12] That translates to about 390 million people who claim to have been healed or to have seen a miracle with their own eyes. Combine this with the fact that Pentecostals tell others about their faith with much greater frequency than other Christians (most do so at least once each week), and we see a powerful force that drives the growth of Pentecostalism. Pentecostal services in India have drawn over one million people at a time, and a Pentecostal church in South Korea has over seven hundred thousand members, making it the largest church in the world of any denomination.[13] More than half the population of the countries of Guatemala, Brazil, and Kenya are Pentecostals.[14] Pentecostal and charismatic Christians have more television and radio stations and shows than any other group of Christians in the world, and they broadcast their healing and miracle stories far and wide to as many people as possible. But eyewitness testimony from someone you know is the next best thing to seeing it yourself, and Pentecostalism has a lot of friendly eyewitnesses.

Conclusion

When I was eight years old, I woke up on Christmas morning to find that my mom, dad, grandma, and grandpa were gone. My aunt told me they were at the hospital because my mom was sick, so we got dressed and spent all day in the waiting room. We found out that she had viral meningitis (an infection of the fluid in the spinal cord and the fluid that surrounds the brain), was in traction, and only had days to live. Our family and friends around the world (even my uncle, aunt, and cousins in Africa) prayed for her. Four days later, she walked out of Parkland Hospital in Dallas, Texas, perfectly healed, and she's been fine ever since.

I've told that story many times—that's exactly how it happened. But while writing this chapter, I looked up viral meningitis and found out that "the illness is usually mild and clears up in about a week" and "fatal cases of viral meningitis are rare, and complete recovery is the rule." What? Then I found that *bacterial* meningitis "is very serious. Severe bacterial meningitis can result in brain damage and even death." Now that's more like it; that's exactly what we were told.

So was it a healing or just an incorrect diagnosis? I've always thought, based on the physician's explanation, that my mom recovered from a deadly infection. Our collective memory of the event certainly includes the threat of death as foretold by the doctor, but maybe what mom had was only "rarely" fatal.

It would not affect the faith of my family or of most Pentecostals to find out that it was not a miracle after all; we would simply have seen it as an honest mistake on the doctor's part and would still have no doubt that healings can and still do happen every day. We would just thank God that he spared her from the worst of the two forms of meningitis. With just such optimism and hope Pentecostalism continues to attract increasing numbers of interested observers and expectant converts. For who knows, maybe miracles really do happen.

CHAPTER 2

WORSHIP AND MUSIC

> Welcome to Pentecostal Headquarters! The Home
> for Positive Pentecostal Experiences! . . . This blog
> is for those who love to have church, and those
> who love church that makes them feel something.
> This site will have hand-clapping, foot-stomping,
> pew-jumping, aisle-running church!
>
> —*Pentecostal Place.com*[1]

In a mountainside barrio near Caracas, Venezuela, fifty-year-old Sister Marlena leads Pentecostal youths in all-night dance, worship, and prayer parties.[2] There are sermons, sodas, sandwiches, and prayers for healing, while the volume elevates throughout the night and the dancing becomes increasingly physical and sensual. There are no alcoholic spirits, only the Holy Spirit, and the sensuality is directed toward God. One of the teenagers, Carmela, testifies that before she met Sister Marlena, she lived for wild drunken parties because her home life was so chaotic and abusive. Carmela and the many other teens like her who come from backgrounds of gangs, drugs, and sexual abuse have found order in their lives with Sister Marlena's parties. The structure is firmly grounded in ecstatic and emotional worship—celebration— and the teens testify that this community actually helps them resist premarital sex. This leads some sociologists to claim that Pentecostalism "is effective in transforming libidinal energies of teens and young adults into the act of worship" and that this may be a significant part of the "unique genius of Pentecostalism."[3]

A friend of mine once commented that the singing in other churches is sometimes like being at a funeral, as if God died and is still dead. As if everybody's pets died too, and Jesus is still on the cross. Pentecostals wonder, "Why is everybody so somber?" Pentecostal worship expresses the feeling and belief that God is alive, Jesus is here with us right now, and we can celebrate! Pentecostal worship does not feel like it's just an ancient faith, thousands of years old; it feels like a faith that is in touch with a living God who is accessible immediately. The vibrant singing and worship reflect this closeness and reality. Pentecostal worship is fun and inviting. It's sometimes more like a rock concert than church. Imagine a rock band cranking out love lyrics to God in a church with all the people singing along, feeling God intimately, with hands raised. If you can imagine that, then you're imagining the Pentecostalization of Christian worship, and it may explain the feelings many people have about Pentecostal worship and music. Pentecostal worship is springing up in places like established and traditional churches too because it is enjoyable.

Pentecostals tend to sing for longer periods of time and repeat the choruses more often than non-Pentecostals. Pentecostals "get into it." When music at a concert is great, the crowds chant, "Encore! Encore!" The musical worship at Pentecostal churches is like calling for an encore and participating in it yourself. Some theologians emphasize that worship is called "liturgy," which means "the work of worship." Pentecostal worship is sometimes work. Standing and singing for an hour or more can be exhausting; people do eventually just want to sit down.

But "the work of worship" is not really a Pentecostal way of describing what they do when they get together to sing, preach, and pray. For Pentecostals, it's more like the *joy* of worship rather than the work of worship. (Compare "the joy of sex" versus "the work of sex.") People who grow up in or begin to visit

Pentecostal churches sometimes feel that other churches stop their songs too soon; just as the feeling starts "getting good," they quit singing! If work is *work,* then it's good to stop, but if work is fun, you want to keep going. If worship—or sex—is good, it lasts longer.

Pentecostal worship music often has drums, electric guitars, horns, pianos, tambourines, and any other instrument that somebody has and wants to play. People clap their hands and move to the music. There's sometimes dancing, there's almost always hugging, and it's OK to connect your head with your heart. The music is often quite professional, and band members even play other gigs outside of church. My cousin Tré was raised in a Pentecostal church, and he plays a mean set of drums. He gets hired to play at other churches, too. So Pentecostal singing and worship is more like the emotion and excitement of a party than a funeral.

"Be not drunk with wine for this leads to debauchery, but be filled [get drunk?] with the Spirit! Speak to one another with psalms, hymns, and spiritual songs. Sing and make music to the Lord."[4] Paul the Apostle's play on spirits and Spirit also helps us think about the ways different Christians worship. Without being judgmental, we can observe that some churches seem not to drink of the Spirit too deeply; others sip daintily from fancy glasses and talk quietly. Pentecostals drink a lot and let loose. They are the ones who claim to drink the most and claim to experience the Spirit most thoroughly. They dance, hug, and tell one another how much they love each other. For them, the church is like a fiesta celebrating what God is doing in the world to redeem it. Worship is partying together.

If the amount of Spirit (or spirits) you drink corresponds to the amount of dancing you do, it seems that some parts of the church are practically teetotalers and don't drink at all, so nary a foot is tapped, a hand clapped, a hug passed, or an "I love you" shared; other parts of the church do all that at the same time! Perhaps there is a continuum along the line of partygoers, from the reserved, mostly silent ones sitting in the corner to the expressive vivacious ones who start the conga line around the room and put the lampshades on their heads. Each is welcome, each is wonderful, and each comes to Pentecostal churches.

Of course, not everyone dances, claps, or weeps. You can if you want, or you can just sit quietly. Conga lines would not be appropriate at some parties, and some parties don't even allow dancing at all. A party that allows both dancing and sitting involves more people, and Pentecostalism is the party where it's OK to drink the Spirit and weep. Such emotional displays "among teetotaling adult males are particularly striking."[5]

But not all Pentecostal music is energetic. The singing and music at Pentecostal worship services tends to start strong and loud; it gets people on their feet, and the energy is high. But after a while the tempo slows, the mood relaxes, and the soothing, peaceful songs flow. Worshipers may sit down or sway gently during the softer, gentler songs. This time of the service is calming, less celebratory, and more relational. The structure of Pentecostal worship is diverse and varied, but it is rarely all high-octane. Like sex, sometimes it's passionate in a "rip my clothes off" kind of way and sometimes passionate in a "tease me slowly" kind of way.

One observer of Pentecostal worship describes it this way:

At Lion of Judah church on Easter Sunday, jubilant sing-ing interspersed with prayer filled the first hour of the service. Celebratory music (backed by a band with drums, flute, saxo-phone, violin, and guitar) gave way to quieter songs, leading up to the sermon. . . . Then came the altar call for those seeking prayers, with gentle music continuing in the background. Ushers with boxes of tissues moved in the aisles, a sign that the praise/prayer segment involved individual as well as collective com-munion with the divine. Music is central to Pentecostal worship and, some say, to its inroads into people's hearts. "Musicologists note that jazz, blues, and other singers talked of going to black Pentecostal churches to learn new riffs, runs, and chords because the style was open to improvisation," says [seminary professor David] Daniels. "The liveliness and jubilance was attractive to many people." Indeed, praise songs and the expressiveness of Pentecostal worship, including the lifting up of hands, has spread through Evangelical churches and nondenominational megachurches.[6]

But Is This in the Bible?

There is plenty of biblical support for expressive, emotional, physical worship, and Pentecostals have gone to great lengths to show it. King David danced so crazily "with all his might" in public in honor of God that he embarrassed his wife because she thought he acted like a lower-class person (2 Samuel 6:1–22). Happy feet, rejoicing in a relationship with Spirit—that's Pentecostalism. Another Pentecostal, Telford Work, feels that Pentecostals "shout back to the Lord what the Spirit has written in our hearts. *Shouting* means not holding back either our joy or our tears. It means not letting either pride or shame tell us how to act. It means giving God our love as outwardly as God gave us his."[7]

Even though Pentecostalism should not be reduced to religious sensuality, its music and worship style show that God is OK with the human body. In fact, God is so OK with the human body that God "incarnated"—God became flesh, meat, human. Incarnation is an important idea when it comes to worship because God became a body, not just a brain. *Dios con carne.* Maybe at a Mexican restaurant you've had *enchiladas con carne* (meat enchiladas) and *sangria* (wine). Christians everywhere eat Jesus' body and drink his blood on Sundays when they take the Eucharist, or as Pentecostals call it, communion. At most Christian churches, you get what was *Dios con carne* (meat God) presented to you as *Dios de pan* (bread God) to eat and *sangria* (wine, from *sangre,* blood) to drink. If you go to some churches, such as the Roman Catholic, or Lutheran, you'll eat and drink God every week; the Eucharist is a significant aspect of their worship.

But Pentecostals don't eat the body and blood of Jesus each week; instead they drink the Spirit (a lot more than a cupful) and use their bodies, their flesh and blood, to worship. Putting a piece of cracker or bread in your mouth, chewing it, and swallowing is a very physical act, and all Christian traditions do this. Jesus said to do it and remember him and "re-member" (put back together) his body, the church. It is also a physical act to clap your hands or raise your arms in the air or to move your feet even a little in time with the music. More than a voice and a brain are involved—your flesh is moving. Moving your body is getting closer to incarnation, for the Spirit has all of you, your whole body—you are *filled* with the Spirit, and all of you, even your emotions and meat, is worshiping God. You are re-membered and made whole as you're put back together. We all are re-membered as we dance and sing together and remember Jesus in our expressive worship. We are physical and emotional beings, not just thinking brains. Pentecostalism creates space for a full human experience, even for people to dance, and God digs dancing.

As David Daniels says, Pentecostals' "exuberant, expressive worship" is about praising with our whole selves. "We are taught that in worship, people are transformed by the Holy Spirit. This healing power and presence of God and the Holy Spirit in worship is extraordinary."[8] Ethnomusicologists, who study music and culture, note that various cultures have "songs that move men to tears."[9] When these songs evoke emotion and transformation, Pentecostals call this the "anointing" and see God at work in the deepest depths of the human soul. These deep emotions come out in physical expression, like King David's dancing.

From the beginning of the Pentecostal movement, there has been the strong belief, based in actual practice and experience, that Pentecostal worship was more accessible, more immediate, more pleasurable, and therefore quite unlike the way many other Christians worshiped and sang. When King David's wife said his dancing was "vulgar" and "common" and "dishonorable,"

David said, "I will celebrate before the LORD. I will become even more undignified than this, and I will be humiliated in my own eyes. But by these slave girls you spoke of, I will be held in honor."[10] The working-class slave girls appreciated David's dancing, but his upper-class wife didn't like it. I don't want to push it too far, but David had been a shepherd (a country boy), so maybe he remembered his working-class background, whereas his wife was the daughter of King Saul, so when she saw him "leaping and dancing before the LORD, she despised him."[11]

Why Pentecostalism's Working-Class Enthusiasm Is Appealing

Most Pentecostals around the world are working-class stiffs, not elites, and that's OK.[12] Rather than try to show that Pentecostalism appeals to all socioeconomic levels of society, even rich folks, I want to encourage us to "hold our horses" and not get carried away with squishing Pentecostals into the dominant classes. We Pentecostals come from the less privileged classes, and our appeal is still among those who work physically hard in unrewarding jobs.

Tex Sample, a working-class Ivy League theologian and sociologist, has done us a great service by showing that upper-class people evaluate and enjoy music differently than working-class people do.[13] His analysis of the tradition and practices of country music among the working class lends itself to exploring the appeal of Pentecostal worship among the workers of the world who are uniting in Pentecostalism. I tried to write this chapter without comparing musical styles and churches, but it couldn't be done; music is a crucial aspect of Pentecostalism and part of its phenomenal appeal.

In the interest of avoiding stereotypes, I must say that there is diversity within the upper and working classes. But Sample's analysis resonates with my working-class upbringing; I hope you find it helpful as well as we look at Pentecostal worship styles through the lens of class. Sample notes that upper-class, elitist tastes and style are distant, detached, disinterested, and indifferent "to the emotional impact of music."[14] They're cool, removed, and "objective"; art is thought to be an end in itself. Although some types of churches have this feel, this is definitely not the way Pentecostals worship or sing. In fact, they intentionally set themselves apart from this way of approaching God.

My wife and I have attended Pentecostal churches almost our entire lives. But we experimented one time and participated in the life of a non-Pentecostal church for a little over a year. We loved the theology and substance of the sermons; we loved the spiritual formation classes for our kids; we loved almost everything about this particular church family. But when they tried to clap while singing, which wasn't very often, they could hardly keep a beat. Deborah would look at me and grin. I would grin and give her the look that says, "Don't make fun of them; they're trying." One Sunday there was a band of about six people who played a variety of African, Native American, and Polynesian drums at the beginning of the worship time. They started slowly and softly with just one drum, patiently bringing in other drum voices and instruments and increasing the tempo and momentum. The intensity built leisurely as the drumming began to penetrate our bodies and reverberate beautifully throughout the sanctuary. The rhythms varied, but the decibel level gradually amplified and complexified until all the drummers together finally brought the song to a crescendoing climax that was absolutely amazing and overwhelming and powerful and exuberant and intense. The response in this non-Pentecostal church? Deafening silence, quiet enough to hear crickets chirping. Not even applause, much less an enthusiastic standing ovation and rapturous participation. I wanted to jump to my feet and clap for them and for God and for the entire experience. But nobody moved. The band quietly walked away from the drums and sat down in the pews. Deborah was shocked at the silence. She leaned over to me in disbelief and said, "If this is all the passion they have in response to that, I can't imagine what they're like in the bedroom." Deborah coined a phrase to describe how she felt coming from a Pentecostal background and being in an academic, cerebral, upper-class church: "a blue-collar girl in a white-collar world." That would make a great country song.

Tex Sample notes that working-class folk critique elites by saying they "'make love with a washrag in their hand,' suggesting that even in the bedroom they had to keep things tidy, neat, and in place and they could not 'let go' even [while having sex]."[15] Surely there is a non-judgmental way of observing that some faiths "let go" more in their worship style. It's not better, just different, and it's growing.

The lyrics of country music show that working-class folk find the elitist class, music, and art "lifeless," "bloodless," and "erotically flat."[16] Working-class taste requires spectator *participation* rather than detachment, and the "pleasures are more intense, direct, and immediate," with high value placed on revelry, laughter, plain talk, immediate satisfaction, and physical reaction.[17] Working-class people feel it and move to it, acknowledging that "we don't fit in with that white-collar crowd; we're a little too rowdy and a little too loud."[18]

Working people "think in proverbs, stories, and relationships more than in propositions, concepts, and discourse."[19] As noted earlier, worship is liturgy—work. And music "works" in different ways. In fact, the common sayings "That doesn't work for me" and "How's that working for you?" show that things we do are put to practical personal use in our lives. Pentecostal worship works for some people; it accomplishes goals and aims that are needed and wanted. And it is of God, for if God truly is on the side of the poor, this is the way God would worship with the working folks. Substituting "Pentecostal worship" for "country music" in the following quote works pretty well:

[Pentecostal worship] as used by working people simply may not be available to people who have not known the working-class world. If one has not worked physically hard; if one has not known dead-end, monotonous, boring jobs; if one has not done such work that must be endured for what happens when one is not working, for which the reward is extrinsic and not intrinsic to the job; if one has not felt the assault of the psychobabble of the university trained on working people whose lives are far more concrete and situationally formed; if one has not listened to highly differentiated language used to comb the innards of the subjective life of the privileged, when such language seems fluff to people who have work and service occupations under close supervision by bosses who do not "give a damn about what they feel"; if one has not done or does not do such things, then [Pentecostal worship] as practiced by working people simply is beyond the world of the privileged, and perhaps beyond their reach.[20]

I would qualify this some; anybody can potentially enjoy a great piano or saxophone solo, but some people are more naturally socialized to be ready for expressive worship.

Sample argues that working-class taste is for things that provide a direct benefit, that do something for you. "It does need to charm, to provide moral example, to be pleasureful, . . . to be agreeable."[21] This is Pentecostal worship well described. Work is boring enough; church doesn't need to be. An article in the *Washington Times* pointed out that "the most common reason people leave church . . . is that it's too similar to their everyday lives."[22] If you have a boring job, why go to a boring church? That doesn't make sense. If you have a boring job, go to an interesting or exciting church.

Some theologians claim that God should be worshiped for God's own sake. But can most people afford such a detached aesthetic? A "what's in it for me?" approach sounds so selfish, but maybe God does want worship to do something for us. We're the ones who live it out every day, who need the joy and strength to make it through. Maybe worship works for God when it empowers and encourages us as we glorify God in praise. My son once said to me, "Daddy, you can't love me as much as you love God because you're supposed to love God the most." That threw me for a minute; then, thankfully, I saw the connection and replied, "Nathan, I love God by loving you. My love for you is love for God." Is it possible that worship that resonates with and inspires regular people also glorifies God, that it works for God most when it works to transform and strengthen God's people? In fact, maybe the theology of worshiping God for God's sake alone is a product of the politics of prestige and distinction. According to that way of thinking, I'm supposed to detach myself from the process and "objectively" focus on conjuring up the goodwill to express to the deity. God is then like an abstract high-end painting on the wall: it's just art, to be admired for what it is. But for Pentecostals, the picture needs to be about something.

Pentecostal worship, like working-class taste, is "rowdy and loud, celebrates in festivity or moans the hard times, revels in active participation and physical enjoyment or laments loss and drowns the blues in [Spirit], that is plain speaking and expressed in hearty laughter or tears and despair, that will often mock and debase elitist expressions and that lets it 'all hang out.'"[23] Judgment has been dished out on the exciting worship of Pentecostalism in pretty heavy doses. For instance, mainline Protestant American missionaries banned guitars and maracas in Latin American churches because the missionaries thought that the instruments were too vulgar and common.[24] But when the missionaries left and the people could lead their own worship, they brought back their guitars, tambourines, and maracas, and the churches thrived and grew. Elitist taste is designed for exclusivity and smallness, and that's what churches like that get—to be exclusive and small. Working-class taste—guitars and maracas—is for the majority of people, and it thrives and fuels Pentecostal growth.

Pentecostals know they're sometimes disrespected and dismissed because of their worship style, and this internalized oppression can be painful. But the worlds that produce Pentecostal worship are valuable, for "in the case of Pentecostal music, the harsh experience of migration produced music that was thematically complex—melancholic, resolute, and joyful at once—and diverse in terms of genre."[25] There is a lot going on in Pentecostal music and worship, yet no genre of music is inherently superior, nor is any genre inherently inferior. Worship style is just culture and taste. Sample puts it this way: "Cultural categories are invented in order to make social inequalities appear 'natural.'" But "people are constantly being typed by their cultural allegiances, respected or dismissed by the music they like. People then internalize these things and believe them about themselves and about the creative capacities of their own traditions."[26] I do want to show that Pentecostal expressive style and taste are equal—different, yes, but equal—to other stylistic manners of worshiping. Perhaps part of the genius of Pentecostalism is that "there may be no two things more powerful in human communication than storytelling and music."[27] Pentecostal music "rocks," and it connects people to the narrative of God through the continual telling of stories (for more on this, see Chapter Five).

Some churches talk about how concerned they are about justice for the poor. There is even the theological belief that God wants justice for the poor. The upper-class denominations rightly want to help working-class or poverty-stricken people; many of those folks worship Pentecostal-style. Again, Tex Sample says that while he pastored a working-class church, he "was concerned about their 'justice issues' but was out of touch with their lifestyle commitments."[28]

Pentecostal worship works like country music, or "white soul." It is appealing because it embodies working-class life and because it makes the ordinary important. Like country music and working-class taste, it "'shows' more than it 'explores.' The concern is not so much to analyze as to display . . . , to give graphic testimony to the necessities, the tribulations, the joys, the struggles, and the ecstasies of concrete lived life."[29] Both workers and Pentecostals are aware of the disdain that others feel toward them and their ordinary lives. One song that relates ordinary life to God particularly well is David Ruis's "Every Move I Make":

> Every move I make I make in you, you make me move,
>   Jesus,
> Every breath I take I breathe in you.
> Every step I take I take in you, you are my way, Jesus.
> Every breath I take I breathe in you.[30]

Sappy as it may sound, my moves, breaths, and steps are intimately related to the way of Jesus. God is walking with me in each part of my day, and I'm never far from God's presence. This is the kind of worship that forms and shapes faithful Christian living during the many hours when we're not "at church." Our ordinary lives of workaday monotony are important to God.

Pentecostal worship is also appealing because it dramatizes and intensifies feeling. Both country music and Pentecostal worship have been called "heart music" that "sings feeling."[31] Sample notes that working-class folk do not "engage in psychobabble on a scale anything like that of college-trained people."[32] Instead, they listen to their feelings as sung by others, and perhaps they sing along. Pentecostal worship music is the kind of music that people listen to all week long—it expresses the feelings that people have for God and for those around them. "Worship" CDs sell by the millions, just like rap, rhythm and blues, and country. To say that people have feelings is to state the obvious. But to recognize that Pentecostal worship expresses those feelings in ways that show they are important is to see the beauty of Pentecostal worship and music. Pentecostal worship seems to affect people in deep and special ways; it touches them. It releases feelings and emotions that are perhaps suppressed or hidden or unacknowledged. Pentecostals create safe environments in which to worship where feelings are honored and respected, where the struggles and ideas and sentiments of working-class folk are not discredited. If you're angry that your son is addicted to drugs or your marriage is on the rocks or your boss is a jerk, you can honestly and powerfully sing in a declarative and commanding way:

I went to the enemy's camp
And I took back what he stole from me,
I took back what he stole from me,
I took back what he stole from me, well
I went to the enemy's camp
And I took back what he stole from me.

He's under my feet
He's under my feet
He's under my feet
He's under my feet
He's under my feet
He's under my feet
Satan is under my feet![33]

Pentecostal worship is an expression of working-class taste and has wide appeal because it is in direct contrast to how "elitist taste legitimates social inequality."[34] Whereas upper-class taste is for those special few with "discriminating" tastes, Pentecostal working-class taste is expressed in music that is, to borrow a phrase, "for us, by us," like the FUBU brand of clothing and shoes designed by African Americans for African Americans. Pentecostals know that all kinds of people like their worship style. But it's not about being fancy or impressing the elites. It's about singing songs and playing music in worship to God in ways that resonate in the deep recesses of the soul. It means working hard and being humble even when you do something well, for "there may be few things in working-class taste as important as being masterful and being one of us."[35]

Latino Music and the Appeal of Pentecostalism

Daniel Ramírez suggests that the explosive growth of Mexican-U.S. borderlands Pentecostalism is significantly due to the way working-class Latino Pentecostals worship with popular music. "Much Pentecostal music reflects an intuitive grasp of the higher critics' notion that the Judeo-Christian scriptures began, after all, as performance, as oral narratives declared . . . in communal settings."[36] As noted earlier, Anglo missionaries preferred "music for high society" rather than "music for the poor" and forbade the use of guitars or maracas in worship because they were low-class instruments. Scholars agree that musical preference has as much to do with class as ethnicity—and elite Christians dismissed "cheapened" music by the poor that was accompanied by instruments such as the accordion ("the instrument of the people"). Even though missionaries and upwardly mobile Christians "distanced themselves from perceived folkways," most people affirmed popular-style music and called the elites *"muy jaitones"* (high and mighty).[37] Working-class *conjunto* music legitimized working-class culture, and on the continuum from Pentecostal music to mainline Protestant music, Pentecostals were the guitar players and maraca shakers. This was the Mexican American version of blues, jazz, gospel, and country—popular music discredited by the elites but embraced by the workers, feeding the spirit of the Pentecostal movement.

Whereas mainline Protestant music split the body from the soul and focused on heady, brainy, disembodied singing, the indigenous (Latino) musical styles embraced the whole body and all the emotions of human experience. This emotional music was condemned because some *gringos* claimed that "music and easy flow of merry words and laughter degenerates into vice. The dancing girl and the wine cup are star attractions [among] pleasure-loving Latins."[38] This quote from the 1920s reflects the prejudice against Latinos at the time, but the exclusion of upbeat music, laughter, and dancing from church services continues to this day. Yet music full of feeling, with a different Spirit, is what breathed life into the church in the twentieth century; the other styles merely pushed working-class Latinos (and working-class African Americans, Anglos, and others) to seek out "freer vocal and aural spaces, spaces found in Pentecostalism."[39] Ramírez notes that people "voted with their ears" and were "as much enchanted by the cultural musical repertoire" of Pentecostal churches as anything else. For in direct contrast to the way upper-class tastes staged a "retreat from folk culture," Pentecostalism recaptured "the *fiesta* of Mexican and Latino culture. . . . Borderlands Pentecostals reintroduced a measure of the carnivalesque (laughter, weeping, body movement, profane instruments, feasts, etc.) into liturgical space and time." Pentecostals found the old hymns lacking and used "popular musical genres . . . to produce a sensory and physical experience."[40]

The story of Filemón Zaragoza, a songwriter and migrant worker in the cotton fields of El Paso, Texas, shows the intimate connection between working and Pentecostal worship. As he prayed during his backbreaking labor, he thought of a worship song and wrote it in the dirt at the side of the field. Throughout the day, he returned to the location to write more lines in the soil and memorize what he was writing. After working all day, he returned across the border to Mexico and rushed to the church, even "before going home to wash the dirt off his weary body," to write the words down on paper.[41] Pentecostal worship songs were written in the dirt of cotton fields by Mexican immigrants—and they are sung by the laborers to God in churches around the world.

> [Pentecostal] musical poetry, emanating from the fields and orchards where many of the songwriters labored, could not help but reflect the contours of the borderlands. Indeed, music captured something of the experience of exhausted bodies dragged in from a day's work, quickly splashed with water and nourished with beans and tortillas before dashing off to the campsite or tent to embrace other bodies in fervent and ecstatic worship.[42]

One can see why Latino Pentecostal musicians were pictured with their "profane and erotic" guitars clearly displayed in the early years of the movement. Although mainline missionaries and their converts refused them, it was "the only instrument available to the working-class church."[43] This led to stories abounding that the music at Pentecostal churches was so good that it alone converted people to the Lord. Although mainline Protestants and upper-class Catholics disparaged Latin Pentecostal *aleluya* music, "the musical culture forged in Pentecostalism's alternative sonic spaces" ultimately did "crescendo and echo in the experience of both popular Catholic and Mainline Protestant believers in Mexico and in the United States."[44] Why is Pentecostalism growing so fast? Because every culture has its popular music, and Pentecostals tend to embrace it.

Jazz and the Appeal of Pentecostalism

We've seen that Pentecostalism is similar to working-class country and Latino music. These styles respond to the dominant forms of music in new and creative ways that reflect working-class tastes and styles. This is also seen in the similarities of blues, jazz, and Pentecostalism. Blues and jazz originated from diverse sources among the same kinds of people at about the same time in history as Pentecostalism. They're multiethnic sisters from the backwoods and the "rough" part of the city. They have global appeal and have influenced others tremendously—Pentecostalism has changed the face of global Christianity, and blues and jazz gave birth to rock and roll. Can you name the poor Pentecostal boy who attended and was baptized in an Assemblies of God church, whose uncles were Pentecostal pastors, and who is the undisputed King of Rock and Roll? That's right, Elvis Presley was a Pentecostal and grew up singing, shaking, dancing, and swaying in black and white Pentecostal churches in Mississippi and Tennessee.[45] But Elvis's Pentecostalism and his rock and roll were preceded by blues, jazz, and earlier Pentecostalism. Exploring blues and jazz will help us see why

Pentecostals have their own unique worship and musical appeal and why it's the world's fastest-growing faith.

Blues "emerged as an acceptable form of self-expression in African American communities of the United States from spirituals, work songs, field hollers, shouts and chants, and rhymed simple narrative ballads. The use of blue notes and the prominence of call-and-response patterns in the music and lyrics are indicative of African influence."[46] When Pentecostals preach, they expect their listeners to say, "Amen!" That's a "call and response." The preacher says something like "Can I get a witness?" And people throughout the audience respond, "Amen, brother!" "That's right!" "Preach it!" I've often heard that "saying 'amen' to a Pentecostal preacher is like saying 'sic 'em' to a dog." Pentecostalism, like blues, has praise songs, hollers, shouts, and chants. Blues came from a context of suffering, and so did Pentecostalism. While others were singing with reserve, slaves were singing the blues; while others were worshiping in straight-back pews, Pentecostals were clapping their hands, tapping their feet, moving to the music, and shouting.

But Pentecostalism is especially like jazz. Jazz "has roots in the combination of Western and African music traditions, including spirituals, blues, and ragtime, stemming from West Africa and New England's religious hymns, and hillbilly music."[47] What a crazy combination—it's a mutt without a pure pedigree. Wynton Marsalis, reflecting on the fact that such an influential style of music came from African Americans, says, "That's how it always is. Cinderella, the one you keep out, and you push down, and you kick, that's the one with the moral authority, with the gift. That's as old as night and day, as old as dust."[48] Preach, Wynton, preach! Pentecostals sometimes feel pushed down and kicked out, and that's one of the places where the musical gifts emerge.

Jazz and Pentecostalism are both strongly African American, but they are also Latino and white, originating among former slaves, immigrants, hillbillies, and city slickers. Think about that: hillbilly country music and African American blues and spirituals mixed with Latino *conjunto*—sounds like Pentecost, where they all worshiped God in their own languages. Jazz is "black musical spirit bursting out of the confines of European musical tradition."[49] Again, it's not that the European musical tradition was bad; it just wasn't complete. There needed to be a bit more diversity. Some would say that's a pretty good description of what Pentecostalism is doing to the church as a whole. The church isn't "bad"; it's just not as diverse as it could be. William Seymour, the African American pastor of the most famous world-influencing Pentecostal revival in Los Angeles in 1906–1908, was the son of former slaves from Centerville, Louisiana, mere miles away from New Orleans, the birthplace of jazz. In fact, a comparison of the history, descriptions, and evolution of jazz to that of American Pentecostalism is truly profound and sheds further light on the appeal of Pentecostalism.

Jazz began in the midst of Jim Crow segregation, poverty, and lynchings in early twentieth-century America in the Deep South, and so did Pentecostalism. Both tried to bring blacks and whites together and succeeded a little bit but couldn't completely overcome the racism of the day. Jazz evoked powerful emotions among both supporters and opponents and was disliked and attacked, according to early critics, because it stirred up people emotionally much more than "older kinds of light music."[50] Historians have said that jazz was "music for expressing strong feelings of dislike" and that in jazz there was no class distinction. It came mostly from poor folk on the bad side of town, and the least privileged and educated could become experts and leaders. Those excluded by the mainstream musical scene actually created powerful music that leads toward the triumph of the popular regular Joe (and Josephine) over the elitist upper-crust.[51] Wow, what a Spirit-filled vision! This idea that the common person matters led to the claim that jazz came "nearer to breaking down class lines than any other art," and since it included the excluded, it obviously had a strong appeal for the oppressed.[52]

Both jazz musicians and Pentecostals also specialize in improvisation. Both jazz lovers and jazz musicians have been known to claim that once you write it down, it is no longer jazz; it has to be improvised *on the spot*. When I was growing up in the Pentecostal church, my pastor actually preached *against* preachers who used notes for their sermons. He opened the Bible and improvised. In fact, in a lot of Pentecostal churches around the world, much of the service is a structured improvisation, just like jazz. And the more structured and less spontaneous a service gets, the less "Pentecostal" it is—there's a real fear that the Spirit won't have room to move if the entire worship time is written down and planned out. A written-down order of worship is not Pentecostal, just as written-down jazz is, according to some, not really jazz.

Some preachers, like jazz musicians, are better improvisers than others; their skill in improvisation completely affects the dynamics of the worship service from beginning to end. I was at a Pentecostal conference recently when Marlon, who was taking up the offering, spontaneously started singing and gestured for the pianist to accompany him so that the audience could join in. He didn't know whether the pianist knew the song (they had just met, and I was later told that they had not discussed it); he was just doing what he felt led by the Spirit to do and was also maybe testing the pianist's improvisational skills. The pianist did fine, even through the key and song changes that Marlon tossed at him, and our spur-of-the-moment worship fit right into the overall structure of the service.

Perhaps this is one reason why there are so many Pentecostals who become great jazz musicians. As far back as 1959, a secular historian noted that "a childhood among the Pentecostal Holiness people or the Churches of God in Christ [black Pentecostal] is so valuable an education for the future jazz musician."[53] Jazz and Pentecostalism both valued unorthodox culture (different can be good), exalted the gifts of the untrained, and specialized in going "straight to the heart of ordinary people."

Both the Pentecostal preacher and the jazz soloist are "hot" and offer the "most concentrated and emotionally powerful" forms of their craft. Since both were unconventional, listening to jazz and attending Pentecostal churches invited scorn from others. Both were forms of social dissent.

This may be why it's so hard for me, as a born and bred Pentecostal, to admire the huge fancy churches that Pentecostals are now building and the quest for acceptability that dampens some of the enthusiastic worship. Sometimes those of us who come from humble beginnings (be they rural or urban) think that when you cross the tracks to the rich side of town, you start to lose the true reality and power of the Spirit. The same happened in jazz—the musicians' feelings of inferiority led to a "yearning for recognition," so they sought praise from classical critics, offered stiff bows, and included violins because the violin was a symbol of sophistication.[54] Pentecostalism and jazz are sisters; there is no doubt about it.

But as distinct as jazz, country, and *conjunto* are, they're still music. They use the same notes that other types of music use; jazz, country, and *conjunto* musicians and singers just do it differently and give it their own unique twist. Music had the potential all along, but it took the right time in history and the right people to produce something so amazing, appealing, and influential. As distinct as Pentecostalism is, it's still Christianity. Most of it is indistinguishable from other kinds of Christianity; Pentecostals are simply worshiping and playing music in their own unique way, which make the church experience especially involving and appealing. Pentecostals are like most people in America and the world; they just happen to be embracing some things that are particularly pleasing to humanity. Pentecostalism isn't completely unusual; it's just peculiar enough for people to sit up, take notice, and maybe start dancing along.

CHAPTER 3

TONGUE-TALKING

Do not forbid speaking in tongues. . . . I speak in tongues more than all of you.

—*Paul the Apostle*

Everybody has a story, and storytelling is as important a part of Pentecostalism as just about anything else. They often call it testifying or sharing your testimony, because it's making public what God has done for you. The diversity of testimonies is as diverse as humanity, and every person's story is different. Testimonies not only make us feel good about God, but they also teach us what we should and shouldn't do, and they can correct hurtful and damaging behavior if we listen carefully.

Michelle reflects the background and experience of the 18 percent of Americans (54 million) who consider themselves Charismatic Christians rather than classical Pentecostals.[1] Here's her story.[2]

I was not raised in a Pentecostal or Charismatic tradition. I came from a mainline-liberal Christian family and as a late teen came to personal faith. African American Pentecostals were among the witnesses used by God to bring me to faith, but I found Pentecostalism too emotionally draining for my personality. I joined the Army and, while stationed in Germany, joined a Baptist congregation.

When I returned to the States, I joined a local Baptist church and found that most of my fellow Baptists—at least in that part of the Baptist world—were very antagonistic to Pentecostals and Charismatics. They believed that the more dramatic gifts of the Holy Spirit, such as healing and especially speaking in unknown tongues, had ceased by the end of the first century. As I began to study the Bible and theology, I realized that their view had very little to recommend it, so I abandoned it.

By this time, however, I had discovered other reasons why my fellow Baptists were anti-Pentecostal and anti-Charismatic. I met Pentecostals who were very immature. Some interrupted funerals to try to raise the dead, causing extreme distress to grieving families. Others insisted that Christians who were not healed of diseases had little faith or had sinned or their family members didn't have enough faith. These kinds of things did little to endear me to Pentecostals or Charismatics. I was also turned off by the anti-intellectualism—which I certainly saw enough of in Baptist circles without importing more. I also found out that during the Charismatic Renewal movement of the 1970s, many immature Charismatics infiltrated Baptist churches and tried to subvert Sunday school classes or whole churches from within, causing many church splits. I may have found no biblical reason to believe that tongues were not for contemporary times, but I was learning many reasons to dislike Pentecostals and Charismatics as I had encountered them.

When I went to seminary, I became friends with a few Pentecostal students who had come to a Baptist seminary instead of one in their own tradition. At about the same time, my younger sister married a man who had come from a Pentecostal church. My new brother-in-law was very nice. But he insisted that salvation was followed by "baptism in the Holy Spirit" and that this was demonstrated by tongue-speaking. Anyone who had not been baptized in the Holy Spirit was a second-class Christian in his eyes.

Well, I was not convinced. In fact, I was persuaded that this phrase was used in the New Testament as another description of salvation or new birth. There are no Christians without the Holy Spirit. However, I still believed that the gifts of the Holy Spirit were available today—and I had seen a few dramatic healings. So I was open but not eager. When a friend asked me why I didn't pray for the gift of tongues, I replied, "Because I have no idea what I would do with it." I understood the practical uses of the other gifts, but not this one.

That's how things stood for some time. Then, several years later, I was a visiting professor at a university. I enjoyed my time teaching there very much, but my spiritual life was in crisis. I have one of those personalities that is prone to depression because of the way I identify with the pain and suffering of the world. (That's one thing that annoyed me about most Pentecostals and Charismatics that I knew—the constant ecstatic joy like someone on drugs and the reaction to any bad news with rebukes about "negative confessions.") A number of personal tragedies hit me and combined with other things to lead to a real "dark night of the soul." I tried to pray for release, but I found myself unable to pray and coming to doubt my entire faith.

I was smart enough to seek counsel from a colleague at the seminary whom I trusted, a philosopher of religion whose views on many things matched mine. He asked me if I had tried contemplative prayer. I knew of the contemplative traditions from seminary and from encounters with Catholic and Orthodox friends. But I told him that I simply had no discipline for this route at the time—silence was killing me because it was leaving me with my own thoughts! He nodded and then said something I never expected: "You should pray for the gift of tongues." Astonished, I asked, "What? Are you Charismatic? Why?"

My colleague explained that intellectual and analytical types like him and me were very prone to overthinking. We can find it difficult to shut off the analytical side and just be in relationship—with other people or with God. He described himself as analyzing every word of a sermon and so not being open to hearing anything from God through that sermon—an experience I had been having for months! (I also found myself doing this with hymns and other things.) There is a place for critical analysis even of sermons and hymns—but while one is trying to worship is probably not the right time! But I had found it impossible to turn off that part of my brain and just worship—or even pray. And this had fed my depression and the doubts about my faith. Glossolalia, ecstatic speech, or tongue-speaking, my colleague explained, bypasses all that.

A light bulb went on in my head. I finally knew a practical purpose for glossolalia. I went back to my office and prayed very simply to receive the gift of tongues, not really believing anything would happen. It came with a rush as real as the wind at the first Pentecost. Suddenly, I was speaking in sounds or words that I did not know and as fast as a babbling brook! Just as suddenly, the presence of God was real and palpable in a way that I had not known in over three years. Tears streamed down my cheeks. I felt loved by Love Himself. My dark night of the soul was over. (I have been able, later, to practice contemplative disciplines from the mystic traditions. I believe these complement rather than stand in tension with ecstatic tongue-speaking as a prayer language.) My subsequent experiences with glossolalia have been very infrequent. Always the gift has manifested itself during a crisis or a time of great personal pain: when I had a miscarriage, when my father died, when personal problems came within an inch of ending my marriage, on 9/11, and when the United States began the "shock and awe" attack on Iraq in March 2003. The experiences have not solved my problems. But they have allowed me to pray and for the Spirit to pray through me in groans that words cannot express (Romans 8:26).

But becoming a Charismatic has been difficult. While I now move in Baptist circles that are less committed to the idea that tongues and miracles have ceased, most of my fellow Baptists still have personal prejudices and bad experiences with Pentecostals and Charismatics. I still would worry that if my Pentecostal brother-in-law learned of my experiences with tongue-speaking, he would try to use it as a club for his arguments with others in the family. He would loudly proclaim that I am now baptized in the Holy Spirit (which I still think refers only to salvation) and would treat me as a better Christian than my non-Charismatic family members. I don't want that. I don't want to be used that way for something I don't believe.

Also, I still find most Pentecostal and Charismatic worship to be emotionally draining. It is hard for me to hit such highs. I have no theological beef with constant praise songs and the like, but I have an aesthetic preference for more formal liturgy. I think this is just the way I'm wired.

Six Things Michelle Teaches Us

Michelle's story shows the beauty and depth, as well as the pain and ugliness, of the belief and practice of praying in tongues. First, tongue-talking is considered weird and odd by many Christians and non-Christians alike. You yourself may have been wondering exactly what it is and why people do it; Michelle provides one good answer to these questions. But ever since the Pentecostal movement began, it's been making headlines for its peculiarities. A front-page story in the *Los Angeles Times* on April 18, 1906, appeared under the headline "Weird Babble of Tongues." The article exclaimed, "New sect of fanatics is breaking loose; Wild scene last night on Azusa Street; Gurgle of wordless talk by a sister."[3]

First of all, admitting that you pray in tongues is kind of like being gay and coming out of the closet: some people take great pride in it and flaunt it, others think it's best just to keep it quiet, and others try to find respectful ways to be who they feel they truly are and live honestly with others who are different. I could hear someone mistakenly identified as a Pentecostal quickly respond, "No, no, I don't speak in tongues—not that there's anything *wrong* with that."

Second, tongues can be a blessing, a gift, a grace to those who pray that way. Sometimes we just don't know the words to say; we don't know how to pray because life can be overwhelming. Poverty, job loss, disease, murder, war, starvation, violence, rape, depression . . . What do you say? Paul the Apostle said, "The Spirit helps our weakness; for we do not know how to pray as we should, but the Spirit intercedes for us with groanings too deep for words."[4] Pentecostals believe Paul was describing a way of praying that we can still practice: when we're broken or hurting or beyond words, the Spirit of God will help us pray, and we don't have to worry about saying just the right thing. All we have are expressions and groans that don't "make sense" but God completely understands.

Third, there are people who pray in tongues who attend a lot of different churches besides the local Assemblies of God or Church of God in Christ. Charismatics who pray in tongues include Catholics, Episcopalians, Mennonites, Quakers, Methodists, and Baptists, to name just a few. The practice is in their Bible, too, and it's the same Spirit. They don't leave their churches; they just pray in tongues. And like Michelle, they're careful whom they tell because it's not always safe. Some are even kicked out for believing or practicing "heresy."

Fourth, Pentecostals are often elitists within Christianity and consider praying in tongues. to be a sign of superiority. I was raised to think that I was the best kind of Christian because I believed in praying in tongues. The famous theologian Paul Tillich said that different kinds of people justify and pride themselves in different ways. There is a pecking order. Rich people have wealth and power; they take pride in that and look down on everybody else. Educated people, the knowledgeable, criticize the wealthy and powerful and take pride in their degrees and wisdom. The professor might say, "I may not have money, but I'm enlightened, and that's what really counts." Religious people condemn the wealthy, powerful, and educated elites by saying, "We may not have money or degrees, but we have God and morality. We're righteous, and that's what really counts."

This pecking order transfers into Christian denominations—a Presbyterian minister in the movie *A River Runs Through It* observed that "a Methodist is just a Baptist who can read."[5] If Baptists were mocked as illiterates, where do you think Pentecostals come in? Far below the Baptists on the status and prestige chart. So we have to get our pride from somewhere, and we found it in what we feel makes us special and Pentecostal—praying in tongues. Presbyterians may have Ph.D.'s and politicians, but Pentecostals have the Spirit and power of God. I am not in any way saying that Pentecostal elitism is justified, but it does make sense. Pentecostal pride in tongues-speech may be overcompensating in unhealthy ways for other perceived shortcomings. But love does not boast, and love is more important than speaking in the tongues of people or angels. It seems that humble, loving Christians who pray in tongues better reflect the scriptural hope and purpose of the gift.

Fifth, people who pray in tongues are not necessarily flamboyant or highly energetic. Some of us may be, but not all of us. Not all African Americans can sing well, not all Asian Americans are good at math, and not all people who pray in tongues jump up and down and run around the church. The most exuberant thing I've ever seen my dad do is calmly raise his hands in the air. Singing style is cultural, and Pentecostals worship and pray in many different cultures: Norwegians, for example, are stereotypically quiet and reserved, while Brazilians are emphatically physical and exuberant. However, Pentecostal worship does, on average, involve more body movement than non-Pentecostal worship. But this does not mean that every Pentecostal is automatically a high-strung, highly caffeinated, bouncy, jolly person.

Sixth, good things can be used to hurt people. Michelle still has not told her family that she prays in tongues. I hope that Pentecostals and Charismatics who read this story will take her experience and concerns to heart and learn humility, not shame. I went from being an arrogant Pentecostal to an embarrassed and shame-ridden Pentecostal to a non-Pentecostal to an anti-Pentecostal—and now I'm just trying to be a faithful follower of Jesus who also prays in tongues sometimes.

Where Did Tongue-Talking Come From?

Praying in tongues is something simple that you can do that has been shown repeatedly, by psychologists, sociologists, and other scientists, to lead to greater personal happiness and a greater sense of personal empowerment. It relieves stress, helps you deal with negative emotions, builds community, and brings about positive transformational change both personally and in society.[6] Hundreds of millions of people in several major religions do it, but Pentecostals do it most of all. Many outside the tradition find it weird or off-putting, threatening, or just plain strange. How can it be that people can begin speaking or praying in a language they've never learned, using words that are not found in any dictionary anywhere on earth?

Tongue-talking is what Pentecostals are most famous for. They've been ridiculed, recorded, and studied because of it. Piles of books have been written about the practice. But most Pentecostals, like most people, tend not to read the scholarly research about who they are. The average Muslim doesn't read textbooks about the history of the globalization of Islam, and the average Catholic doesn't read what social scientists are saying about Roman Catholicism. They live their lives and practice their faith. In the same way, Pentecostals just pray in tongues for their families, friends, finances, health, jobs, churches, missionaries, politicians, and anything else that they feel needs prayer. They are glad to say that it makes them feel better, happier, and more joyful because they are helping. It also sustains them during challenging times of suffering and despair because it helps them communicate with God even when life is difficult. Pentecostals know this from experience, and scientists have verified it. But where did this crazy-sounding practice come from?

The Jewish feast of Pentecost comes fifty (*pente* in Greek) days after the feast of Passover, one of the major Jewish holidays and the time during which Jesus was crucified. At Pentecost fifty days after Christ's death, his followers were "filled with the Holy Spirit" and spoke in languages they did not know—or at least were heard in languages they did not know. The book of Acts says, "When the day of Pentecost arrived, Jesus' followers were in an upstairs room praying together. Suddenly the room where they were praying was filled with the sound of a mighty rushing wind, flames of fire appeared to be on each of their heads, and they all were filled with the Holy Spirit and began to speak in languages they had never learned as the Spirit enabled them."[7] People from all over the Mediterranean world heard these followers of Jesus talking in their own native languages about how wonderful God is. And that's why Christians who speak in tongues today are called Pentecostals.

But there's another part to the story. As the book of Acts tells us, the people outside the prayer meeting room thought Jesus' followers were drunk. But the Apostle Peter explained to the crowd that instead of being full of spirits, they were full of the Spirit, and this was a fulfillment of God's plan for all humanity—sons and daughters, old and young, even both female and male slaves! Peter then told the story of Jesus' life, death, and resurrection and invited all the people listening to "change your lives. Turn to God and be baptized, each of you, in the name of Jesus Christ, so your sins are forgiven. Receive the gift of the Holy Spirit. The promise is for you and your children, but also to all who are far away."[8] About three thousand people—including Arabs, Asians, Egyptians, Romans, and Libyans (all Jews)—accepted Peter's message that day and started learning, eating, sharing, and spending time together.

But tongue-talking did not stop after that first Christian Pentecost. It continued, and both Acts and the Apostle Paul tell us that it became a regular part of early Christian worship. Paul even claimed, to a group of Christians who were proud of how much they spoke in tongues, "I praise God that I speak in tongues more than all of you!"[9]

However, tongue-talking consistently went together with talking about Jesus and helping people follow him better. A commander in the Roman army and his entire family were listening to Peter tell them about Jesus over dinner one night when "the Holy Spirit came on all of them. . . . Peter and the others were shocked that the gift of the Holy Spirit had been poured out even on non-Jews! For they heard them praying in tongues and praising God."[10] Peter then had to explain this unexpected event to the unsuspecting Jewish Christians back in Jerusalem: "As I was speaking, the Holy Spirit came on them as he had come on us at Pentecost. Then I remembered what the Lord had said: 'John baptized with water, but you will be baptized with the Holy Spirit.' So if God gave them the same gift as he gave us, who believed in the Lord Jesus Christ, who was I to think that I could oppose God?"[11] What could they say to that? They had no further objections and praised God that even all the Gentiles of the world could also follow Jesus and be empowered by the Spirit—and speak in tongues.

Nudity, Love, and Tongues: Tongues in Private and in Public

Nudity can be beautiful and awe-inspiring, or it can be awkward and embarrassing; it can be glorious, and it can be downright degrading—it depends on the context. The majority of us don't cover our faces with clothing, but we do put pants on our bottoms most of the time. And just because we cover our private parts certainly doesn't mean that we wish we didn't have them. Life would be a lot more painful and a lot less fun without them; they're rather important and indispensable. We could say that we give our very special private parts a unique honor by covering them.

You are probably naked alone more than with others, and whenever you go out of your house to be with friends, you probably put on clothes. You treat your special parts with special honor; you're careful with them and how you show them off. Paul the Apostle actually used a similar analogy to refer to praying in tongues around other Christians and non-Christians at church. He said it this way: "Those parts of the body that seem to be weaker are indispensable, and the parts that we think are less honorable we treat with special honor. And the parts that are unpresentable are treated with special modesty, while our presentable parts need no special treatment."[12] Pentecostals use this passage to illustrate how we should treat praying in tongues. Scripture teaches that praying in tongues is not the most essential gift, but since it is important and has its place, we must treat it with special modesty. This means we don't show it off by disrupting a service with our ability to pray in tongues or interrupt others by praying in tongues.

Did you know that one of the most famous verses in the Bible was written about the gift of tongues? "Love is patient, love is kind. It does not envy, it does not boast, it is not proud. It is not rude, it is not self-seeking, it is not easily angered, it keeps no record of wrongs . . . it bears all things, always trusts, always hopes, always perseveres. Love never fails."[13] You hear this often at weddings, and that's nice. When Paul wrote this, he was referring specifically to spiritual gifts, and most specifically to Christians praying in tongues at church. In fact, this celebrated passage on love starts after this rhetorical question: "All do not speak in tongues, do they? All do not interpret, do they? But eagerly desire the greater gifts. And now I will show you the most excellent way. If I speak in the tongues of people and angels, but have not love, I am only a bothersome gong or a clanging cymbal."[14]

Many first-century Christians had the idea that praying in tongues showed that they were especially spiritual and godly. They could, after all, speak in unknown languages through the power of the Holy Spirit. Paul thought that any tongue-talking had to be done in love (it does not boast, it is not proud, rude, self-seeking, and so on). Otherwise, it was irritating, distracting, and just plain offensive. Talking in tongues and interrupting a church service for your own good feelings is like mooning everybody. Bragging about being able to speak in tongues is naively arrogant and like bragging about your private parts. The gift may be good, but you don't need to show it off.

Paul explicitly linked love and praying in tongues. He told those "misinformed" Christians that "these three remain: faith, hope, and love. But the greatest of these is love. Follow the way of love *and* eagerly desire spiritual gifts, especially the gift of proclaiming the truth. For anyone who speaks in an unknown tongue does not speak to people but to God. No one even understands them! . . . The person who speaks in tongues feels good and builds himself or herself up, but the person who proclaims the truth strengthens everybody else too."[15] Love is not selfish. Love is not most concerned about itself and making itself feel or look good. Love thinks about others and seeks their good. Applying the way of love to tongue-talking when believers come together creates an open, giving, and amazing atmosphere where the voice of God can be heard. But Paul was wise enough to know that praying in tongues, like any other part of human behavior, can be misused or flaunted or subverted to our egos.

I vividly remember the time my three-year-old son sneaked up on the platform after a church service, found the drumsticks, and started thrashing on the cymbals. It was cute but annoying. He was grinning from ear to ear, but he was not really making music; he was making noise. Saint Paul told his friends in Corinth, who were so caught up in public tongues-speech, that doing it without interpreting it—saying it again in a language that everybody else could understand—was like blowing crazily through a flute or trumpet or slapping a harp.[16] It may be fun, but it's noise like my son made banging on the cymbals; it's not music that the rest of us can appreciate. Last Christmas, my nephew got really happy and started banging on the piano keys. He was laughing, enjoying the sounds he was making—it was an expression of his abundant and overflowing joy. But it got annoying really fast.

This illustrates the difference between private praying in tongues and public praying in tongues—which *always* needs to be restated in the vernacular (English in English-speaking cultures). Saint Paul's request for an interpretation of public tongues-speech is like asking that after a kid bangs on the piano, playing notes that make no sense, somebody else should go play a song on the piano that we can all enjoy and appreciate. Speaking in tongues is fun noisemaking; the interpretation is a song we can all understand.

Praying in tongues by yourself, though, is very different from praying in tongues in public, at church. When you're alone, you can bang on the piano or practice the drums all you want, and you and God can just enjoy it together, no worries. You can take your clothes off and nobody cares. God doesn't mind. So tongues-speech when Pentecostals are alone—as when Michelle was alone in her office—does not need to be interpreted. It is for the person praying and God.

But when you're with other folks, think about their ears, eyes, minds, hearts, and souls. Play notes that uplift them, and keep your clothes on. Speak in tongues wisely, carefully, respectfully, with awareness and the intention that your prayer be interpreted into the language of those present. This is the way of love. Paul said he spoke in tongues more than all the tongues-addicted believers in Corinth, but he then made his real point: "But in the church I would rather speak five intelligible words to instruct others than ten thousand words in a tongue."[17]

If people come to our times of fellowship and we are banging on pianos and running around naked, they will, quite understandably, think we're crazy. "If everyone speaks in tongues and inquirers or unbelievers come in, won't they think you're out of your mind?"[18] Yes, Paul, they will. So all tongue-speaking in public, with others around, should be done "for the strengthening of the church." That means it should be interpreted, and "if there is no interpreter, the speaker should keep quiet in the church and speak to himself and God."[19]

Last Sunday, my family and I attended a Mennonite church. There are Pentecostal and Charismatic Mennonites there, but as far as I know, the congregation does not usually experience people speaking in and interpreting tongues during Sunday morning worship, and I wasn't about to do so. But the songs we were singing were so beautiful and so powerful and the time for prayer for healing was so inspiring—the pastors came to the front and then all who needed prayer for any reason lined up in the center aisle and came forward in turn—that I could not help but weep and pray in tongues. I did so quietly, however, as an almost unvoiced whisper. Nobody around me even knew that I was praying in tongues, but I was worshiping and enjoying the presence of God as I sat peacefully in my pew.

Early Christians spoke in tongues when they came together for worship, and we know that they spoke in tongues in their private prayer times as well. But Paul, and presumably other leaders, had to rein in their public exuberance while still encouraging them to be open to God's gift of praying in tongues. He summed up his advice like this: "Three things, then, to sum this up: When you speak forth God's truth, speak your heart out. And don't forbid praying in tongues, but be courteous and considerate in everything."[20]

Why This Appeals to So Many People

About 40 percent of Pentecostals say they never speak or pray in tongues. This means that more Pentecostals claim to have witnessed or experienced a miracle than claim to have spoken in tongues. But why is it so appealing for the 60 percent—360 million people—who do speak in tongues? I think there are at least six good reasons.

First, it happened in the Bible, so it's OK. The New Testament gives good examples to follow, bad actions to avoid, and specific teachings to learn from. Jesus baptized his followers with the Holy Spirit, and lots of early Christians spoke in tongues.

Second, it's cleansing and emotionally purging. While I was in college, my dad was stalked and threatened by one of his employees for a while (yes, he worked for the United States Postal Service). I would go to the school chapel when it was empty, lay face down on the carpet, and pray in tongues, releasing my fear and concern for my dad. As a fellow Pentecostal explains, "When there is a lack of words to communicate what is going on in my life, it's time to just pray in tongues and let go. I don't have to categorize and classify everything. . . . So praying in tongues allows me to pray without having to know. I can just pray—God knows everything. It releases me from stressing myself out."[21] A tongue-talking philosopher, James K. A. Smith, says that privately praying in tongues is "deeply cathartic and represents a kind of spiritual discipline."[22] And this spiritual discipline—a practice by which we learn to be friends with God and others—is also deeply therapeutic. *Therapy* comes from a Greek word that means "to heal," and praying in tongues often brings healing and helps maintain spiritual and emotional health.

Third, it's intimate. A Pentecostal who was interviewed in Atlanta said, "I do it as much as I can and as often as I can. I find that it edifies me. The Bible says to use tongues to edify yourself—to build yourself up. So sometimes I will pray just to build my spirit up. What I have said when I speak in tongues, I have no idea. I feel something spiritual and supernatural happens in my spirit that just builds me up."[23] Some people don't believe in God, and that's understandable. But if you do believe in God, why not have a conversation when you speak to God? And if you're out of words or would like to pray in a way that connects deeply with your whole being (not just the language-making part of your brain), praying in tongues is about as emotionally revealed as you can get. Moments of real connection with God are what can happen when you pray in tongues—it's a wordless but still verbal way of communicating with the essence of all reality (otherwise known as God).

Fourth, it feels real. Humans are emotional beings, and Pentecostalism allows for and encourages emotional interaction with God. People all over the world express their emotions differently, but kids everywhere love to clap, jump, sing, and dance (unless they've been socialized away from doing so). Glossolalia gives voice to deep, almost primal parts of human experience. Music does this too. Whether it's classical, rock, metal, jazz, blues, pop, reggae, or country, if we like it, it moves us. And we often feel different (usually better) while and after listening to our favorite songs. Studies of tongues-speakers have consistently shown that they are *not* psychologically abnormal, and it is generally agreed by non-Pentecostal researchers that people who pray in tongues are not in a trance, and that they are in control of the experience. There is a growing consensus that praying in tongues has a lot "in common with the altered states of consciousness experienced while listening to music"; it's like being "in the flow" or "in the groove."

Fifth, James Smith also thinks that tongues-speech is more about doing something than saying something.[24] So perhaps it's a protest and worship language that is socially empowering, especially for the downtrodden and oppressed. Studies have shown that Pentecostals in neighborhoods and cities with higher rates of poverty, crime, and addiction pray in tongues "frequently each day as they are walking, driving, shopping, and going about other daily tasks and chores."[25] Here's another testimony:

> There are times that I have seen stuff happen—tragic stuff—that the only thing I can do is pray in tongues. When the mind says, "You are not going to make it," but the supernatural says that I am praying in tongues because there is nothing I can do in the natural world that will change what God's outlook will be. It's a way that God gives us to communicate with him so that the peace we have inside of us can come around full circle. It gives me a peace

about whatever happens—any situation, whether it is good or bad. I communicate with God on a level I cannot understand, and it gives me peace about whatever is going on.[26]

Sixth, praying in tongues opens people up to the spiritual "in-between," the kind of life and reality where amazing things can happen. The experience of tongues-speech changes how you see the world. When I was a senior in college, I spent the summer in Nuevo Casas Grandes, Mexico, helping start a new church. We visited people every day and held services every night in a big yellow-and-white tent on a dusty corner lot.

While praying in tongues along with scores of others one night, I felt very strongly that I should make my way through the crowd and pray for a little two-year-old girl with limp legs who could not stand or walk. Her mother had brought her to every service hoping that she would be healed. I knew that if I prayed for her, everybody would be watching, and I was nervous. But the more I prayed in tongues, the more certain I felt that I should do it. But I put a condition on it: I silently told God that my friend who was praying next to me had to say "do it" in order to confirm that what I was feeling was truly from God. After a couple of minutes, I stopped praying, tapped Mark on the shoulder, looked him in the eye, and slowly asked, "Do you have a word from God for me?" He looked at me, paused, and said, "Do it."

Immediately, I turned and walked through the crowd at the front of the tent and found the mother and her little girl. I held out my hands and asked her if I could pray for her daughter. She tenderly handed the girl to me. I held her gently and prayed as best I could, and many others joined in, praying in tongues and asking God to heal this baby. I had been taught that after praying, we should see if what we'd prayed for had happened. So I held her under her arms, got down on my knees, and carefully placed her feet on the dirt floor. When I could feel that her legs were beginning to support her weight, I released my hands from under her arms and held her hands. As she hesitantly stood there, wobbling a little, I let go of her hands and let her fingers hold my fingers instead. I can't tell you what was going on around me, what her mother was doing or anybody else. All I can remember is that little girl right there in front of me and the feel of her grasping my fingers and standing without me holding her up. She did not walk; she did not take even one step. She just stood there holding my fingers. After what couldn't have been more than about thirty seconds, I picked her up, hugged her, and handed her back to her mom, who was smiling as tears rolled down her cheeks.

My actions in this instance were supported by the nature of the service itself (praying for healing was OK), but I specifically and spiritually *felt* encouraged, compelled, and invited by God to pray for that particular girl. Pentecostals consistently testify that while praying in tongues, they think about things they're not usually open to, and then sometimes they even act on the insight or idea that they have.

Conclusion

Unknown tongues are the language of the heart and soul, not just the head, and they're connected to action. Tongues issue from the depths of the human experience and open up new ways of living, being, and doing. A teenaged Pentecostal from Atlanta gets the last word:

> One day I was sitting on the floor praying in tongues. I was the only one on the floor and could see everyone's feet. I heard God say, "Do you want me to show you power? You heard how Jesus healed leprosy and all that kind of stuff?" I said, "Yeah, that would be neat." I saw that one guy had pretty messed-up feet. I wondered if I would lay hands on him—whether his feet would be healed right there. I got stirred up. So I got up and went over to him and began praying, really praying. Something overtook

me, and I started praying in tongues. Then I took this man's feet in my hands! That's something I never expected to do. I thought I could never do it, but I did it and was filled with love for this guy. I felt love for somebody I didn't even really know! I didn't know what kind of disease he had—and I didn't care. When I finished praying, nothing happened. The guy's feet were still messed up, and I was kind of discouraged. So after a couple of days, while I was praying, I said, "You know, God, you told me power and all that stuff. What did you do? You were going to show me power, and I didn't see anything." God said, "It wasn't about healing; it was about the power of love. You did something that you thought you would never in your life do. You did it for love—the love that I put in your heart. It is so powerful you can do anything. People that you thought were human garbage, now you almost kiss their feet. You are loving them. They are your brothers. *That is powerful.* It makes you do stuff that you think you would never be able to do."[27]

CHAPTER 4

PROSPERITY (OR MONEY, MONEY, MONEY, MONEY)

I must tell you boldly: God wants to make you rich.

—*Robert Tilton*

Pentecostal prosperity preachers on television shows and from behind pulpits around the world claim that a $10 gift will yield $1,000. As Gloria Copeland, one of the main proponents of the prosperity gospel, has claimed, "You give $1 for the gospel's sake and $100 belongs to you. You give $10 and receive $1,000. Give $1,000 and receive $100,000. Give one airplane and receive an equivalence of ten airplanes."[1] She should know; she and her televangelist husband have a $6 million mansion and a $20 million jet.[2]

It is common for both preachers and practitioners of the prosperity message to say things like "Receive your miracle!" and "If you have a need, plant a seed." This is sometimes known as "seed faith." You show your faith by giving money—plant a dime to reap a dollar, or tip your bellboy to bring you the car that you want—God is your ultimate errand boy. Of course, planting a seed means giving dollars to a particular minister. And the thousandfold return is a miracle, not simply the result of prudent investing or financial planning. These preachers teach that the poor are poor because of sin in their lives and a lack of faith. Therefore, if they would quit sinning and have more faith, they could be wealthy. They use the terminology of "claiming" to try to get what they want.

One of my colleagues often says, "I am *not* claiming that" when someone mentions something negative. In a discussion about the downturn in the economy and the real possibility of recession, she said, "The Bible says God wants us to be prosperous, so I'm not claiming that." But when she sees something she desires, she says, "I'm claiming that in the name of Jesus." She often hosts prosperity gospel Bible studies at her desk. At one of them, another woman said, "I want a car." My colleague asked, "What kind do you want? Do you want leather seats? What luxuries do you want? You name it, and it's yours." When the woman answered that she wanted a white Honda Accord, she was instructed, "Just claim it every day. The next step is thanking God for it. Thank God in advance every day for already giving it to you. It's yours; you've claimed it. When you go outside every morning and it's not there, keep claiming it and thanking God for it." Eventually the woman did get her car. When asked about the details of how it worked out for her, she told us that she actually had taken out a loan, so she now had a monthly payment like most other car owners. Such requests are generally geared toward luxury, and the received promises are usually about as miraculous as taking out a loan.

This message emerges in large part from the Reverend Norman Vincent Peale (1898–1993) and his theology and psychology of the power of positive thinking. Peale was one of the most influential clergymen in the United States during the twentieth century and was the pastor of Marble Collegiate Church in New York City for fifty-two years. In *The Power of Positive Thinking* (which has sold over twenty million copies in forty-two languages) and his dozens of other books, he taught that the unconscious mind has a "power that turns wishes into realities when the wishes are strong enough." This wishful-thinking-becoming-reality is precisely what Pentecostals picked up on and juiced up by applying the power of the Holy Spirit to money. Peale himself taught that "through prayer you . . . make use of the great factor within yourself, the deep subconscious mind. . . . Positive thinking is just another term for faith."[3]

Although Peale had been ridiculed for his motto "Change your thinking, change your life," Pentecostal televangelists including Oral Roberts and Kenneth Copeland took it and ran with it. Peale's books had titles like *You Can Win!* and *Reaching Your Potential*, and Pentecostal prosperity gospel folks write books with titles like *God's Will Is Prosperity* and *God's Success Formula*. Copeland claims that it "is God's will for you to prosper in every area of your life: spiritually, mentally, physically, financially, socially and more!" and that "The anointing to prosper comes on the obedient people of God" who speak it into existence with positive confessions of wealth and riches.[4] "The financial anointing . . . means that God can work in a miraculous ways" because Christians who believe they'll be rich and say it in faith "shall spend their days in prosperity and their years in pleasure. . . . God is calling the church back to wealth."[5] Wanting a positive and prosperous life is not a uniquely Pentecostal idea, but claiming it as a guaranteed blessing from God for those who can conjure up the positive confessions and prayers to get it is.

Pentecostals and Money: Contemporary Manifestations

In this world of drastic widespread poverty and wealth accumulation unparalleled in history, the Pentecostal prosperity message of money, money, money, money might seem to ring hollow. Ron Sider's best-seller *Rich Christians in an Age of Hunger* challenges Christians to hoard less and work for political change to alleviate suffering.[6] However, the Pentecostal prosperity gospel appeals to *hungry* Christians in an age of wealth and proclaims that if you have faith in God, you will be financially secure. Over 90 percent of Pentecostals and Charismatics in Nigeria, South Africa, India, and the Philippines believe that "God will grant material prosperity to all believers who have enough faith."[7] And in every country, significantly more Pentecostals than other Christians believe this.

This teaching is based on an interpretation of Malachi 3:10–12 that is applied directly to the lives of believers. "Bring the whole tithe into the storehouse, that there may be food in my house. Test me in this, says the LORD Almighty, and see if I will not throw open the floodgates of heaven and pour out so much blessing that you will not have room enough for it. I will prevent pests from devouring your crops, and the vines in your fields will not lose their fruit."[8] As one prosperity preacher says, "God has already made provision for his children to be wealthy here on earth. When I say wealthy, I mean very, very rich. . . . Break loose! It is not a sin to desire to be wealthy."[9] The two crucial elements are faith and giving. When combined, they allow you to reap a "harvest of a thousandfold," or at worst a hundredfold return. If a Christian has enough faith to go along with the practice of tithing (giving at least one-tenth of your income to the church), then she can unlock the money dam of heaven and be blessed with cars, bursting bank accounts, employment, and even fertility.[10] Prosperity gospel proponents claim that Jesus' victory over death brings Christians victory over debt and poverty. They claim that Jesus' riches in heaven bring Christians riches on earth, that we can receive the spiritual resources that guarantee abundant financial success. Wealth then is a consequence of God's promises and of Jesus' life, death, and resurrection. They think that when Jesus said, "Give it and it shall be given to you, pressed down, shaken together, and running over" (Luke 6:38), he was definitely talking about Christians accumulating lots of money. With such a great message, it's no wonder people are flocking to sign up.

The prosperity gospel is a divinely guaranteed version of the American dream: a house, a job, and money in the bank. And the global success of the prosperity gospel is the exporting of the American dream: to have enough (and then maybe a little bit more). Although Pentecostals believe that their faith in God is a key to their financial success, a recent poll shows that they also believe that "hard work," "education," "government policies," "personal connections and contacts," and "people's parents' economic situation" are crucial as well. In fact, American Pentecostals consider each and every one of these other variables more important than other American Christians did, as well as American citizens as a whole.[11] This means that although Pentecostals tend to believe that faith in God yields economic success, such things as the people you know, how hard you work, and how much money your parents have matter too. In fact, Pentecostals agree that hard work and going to school matter as much as "faith in God."[12] Hence the oft-heard saying among Pentecostals whose children go off to university or seminary: "Get your learnin', but don't lose your burnin'!" In other words, go to college, but stay on fire for Jesus. Have faith, and get to know the right people.

Perhaps rather than the American dream, the prosperity gospel is the African dream. African theologians argue that the African worldview is holistic and that African primal spirituality is concerned with the whole of life and the unity of the human race and that salvation includes life on earth.

Lawrence Nwankwo and I were drinking coffee at a café in Belgium after a conference about Pentecostals and ethics. Lawrence, who is from Nigeria, was telling me that God wants all Christians to be prosperous. A bit embarrassed by the money-hungry theology we American Pentecostals had exported to Africa, I wanted to offer (in a humble and thoughtful way) what I thought was a correction. I told him that God does not want us to be rich; he wants us to live simply and be generous with all that we have. Food, clothing, shelter, health care, and education—these things are necessary and important, but prosperity for all is impossible. It's not true, I said, that God wants everybody to be wealthy. In my American context, I had seen materialism and consumerism all around me. I felt like I was surrounded by a bloated, greedy church that seemed to lust after more and more possessions, spending what it did not have on things it did not need to impress people it did not like. I did not like the prosperity gospel, and I didn't think it was a good thing for it to spread into Africa. As a Pentecostal, I have had more than my fill of "God wants you to be rich" preaching. Name it and claim it, blab it and grab it—it doesn't matter what you call it; I actively teach against it. From my self-righteous perch, I told my African friend that prosperity teaching had always been and would always be a heresy.

Lawrence smiled and patiently reiterated that God wants us to be prosperous, to have plenty. He explained that the Bible clearly teaches prosperity. I shook my head and said that prosperity was not biblical and could not be justified theologically or practically; he countered that prosperity was completely biblical and right for Christianity and the world today. After about half an hour of this and several cups of coffee, we began to see each other in our respective contexts, and it slowly dawned on us that we were saying the same thing. The word we were using, *prosperity*, had confused us.

I was arguing against overabundance, hoarding, greed, exorbitance, and consumerism—and *for enough for a healthy life*. I argued for a *simple* existence. He was arguing against starvation, poverty, sickness, and hopelessness—and *for enough for a healthy life*. He argued against subsistence and for a simple *existence*. I was looking up the mountain of money and trying to bring the wealthy down; he was looking down into the valley of despair and trying to bring the poor up.

Lawrence says that Africa's holistic worldview means that "the expectation that the experience of wholeness, that is long life, wealth, fertility, success, etc., is legitimate and that religion should contribute to its provision."[13] He points to the Igbo people of southwestern Nigeria as a good example of this and as an explanation of why prosperity teaching strikes a deep chord in Africa. The Igbo understand their gods to have an obligation to provide the conditions for well-being in the lives of the people in the community—life on earth is a foretaste of the fullness of life in the "other world." So the prosperity gospel is really a human dream—to have enough (and maybe a little more).

The Problems with Prosperity

The first problem with the prosperity message is that there are no guarantees that financial miracles will occur unless the community works together and provides. The prosperity gospel hurts and deceives a lot of people, draining them of their limited resources and alienating them.

Lucia (not her real name) watched prosperity gospel television and prayed and wept all night long. Her husband was unfaithful and her marriage was in shambles, her dressmaking business was about to close, and she suffered from depression. Things finally got so bad that she visited the Pentecostal church, whose pastor promised "the more you give, the more God will bless you." Lucia lived in a slum in Rio de Janeiro, Brazil, and since she believed this pastor, she began to give one-half of her income to the Universal Church of God's Kingdom, which is one of Brazil's most popular denominations. The church has a millionaire pastor and a billion-dollar budget. However, a year later, her marriage was still a disaster, her business was still weak, and she had not recovered from her depression. She decided to leave the church because even though she gave most of her income just like the preacher said, her problems remained. "You think that if you give, everything in your life will be resolved, but it resolved nothing for me. I still believe in God, but I don't believe in any church, and I don't believe in pastors. Now, when I have problems, I solve them myself."[14]

The Universal Church of God's Kingdom reportedly has ten million members and owns Brazil's third most popular television network. It also owns a bank and several dozen radio stations and newspapers. Getting your message out is just good evangelism (and good business), so TV, radio, and newspapers are ways of distributing it. But churches owning banks? What message is this distributing? The prosperity gospel has been called a "spiritual version of Wall Street" and is accused of playing to people's greed. And that is the second problem, for a few get rich off the message and yet their greed seems never to be satisfied.

Robert Tilton, a Pentecostal televangelist, testified in court that he was making $800,000 per month (that's $9.6 million per year) and was living on a $450,000 yacht.[15] Yet ABC-TV's *Prime Time Live* reported that he was actually bringing in closer to $80 million per year. He promises his television audience, "I must tell you boldly: God wants to make you rich. . . . God wants to make a millionaire out of certain ones who receive this letter. Is it you? I want you to put a checkmark on the back of the Million Dollar Bill [that he had mailed out] of what you need or desire, and send it back to me, along with a Seed Faith Gift of $200. . . . This ministry has given you spiritual food, so it's time to pay your tithes."[16] Doing this in the name of God makes it worse than when regular corrupt businesses do the same thing. It is taking God's name in vain in one of the worst ways—for greed—and thereby desecrating the third commandment. As Tulsa attorney Gary Richardson says, "The people that these guys so often attract are people that are going under for the third time. If you looked up and saw a straw on the surface of that water, you would still reach for the straw."[17] Tilton is still going strong, selling his books and CDs, bearing such titles as *How to Be Rich and Have Everything You Ever Wanted*, and he recently built a 12,000-square-foot home on an island in Biscayne Bay near Miami Beach, Florida.[18]

This is why not all Pentecostals agree on the prosperity gospel, and recognizing the diversity is important. Classical Pentecostal denominations such as the Assemblies of God officially teach against positive confession and the prosperity gospel. Positive confession is what my colleague did when she would "name it and claim it" in the name of Jesus. She confessed positive things to bring them about. The Assemblies of God asks rhetorically, "Does the [prosperity gospel] teaching have meaning only for those living in an affluent society? Or does it also work among the refugees of the world? The truth of God's word is as effective in the slums as in suburbia. . . . It is as effective among the deprived nations as among the affluent."[19] But still the prosperity gospel thrives. While a billion people in the world live on less than $1 per day and three billion live on less than $2 per day, the top 20 percent of the world (which probably includes me and you) consume 86 percent of the world's resources, while the poorest 20 percent share just 1.3 percent of the world's resources. Does God want that many people to suffer that way? One billion people sharing 1 percent of the earth's produce? I'm going to go out on a limb here and say no. The world is full of suffering; that is a fact. God should care; that is a fact. The prosperity gospel combines these two facts into a preachable theology of economic hope that has the potential to take a struggling widow's last dollar.

Another difficulty is that people who have plenty are taught by marketers not to be satisfied or content, so people with more than enough can still want more. Prosperity teaching exacerbates this problem when it emphasizes exorbitance by linking greed with God's blessing.

Yet even though the prosperity gospel often appeals to people's greed, Lucia's desire for a stable marriage, a successful business, and good mental health is not greedy or evil; offering false promises and cashing in on her pain is. Paul warned in First Timothy that "people who want to get rich fall into a temptation and a trap." And Jesus warned of the "deceitfulness of wealth," saying that the good word of God is choked and dies in people who seek riches. Prosperity preachers should sell their Rolls-Royces and Bentleys, recognize that they are prosperous without them, and help bring true prosperity to the people they have been deceiving.

One of these preachers has done just that. Benny Hinn is a Pentecostal televangelist who preaches to hundreds of thousands of people. One of his trademark moves is to swing his coat around and around over his head to "unleash the power of the Spirit," which purportedly knocks people over by the thousands. He eventually repented of his get-rich preaching after years of peddling the prosperity gospel. He said, "It promotes greed when we tell people that if they give $10 they'll get back $1,000. I feel terrible that I once put too much emphasis on material prosperity, and now I am saying Lord, please forgive me."[20] He had a change of heart when some other Pentecostal leaders talked with him about the teaching. It's admirable that he changed his theology and teaching, and it shows that there are healthier ways to preach biblical prosperity.

The Promise and Appeal of the Prosperity Gospel

"Give me neither poverty nor riches, but give me only my daily bread. Otherwise, I may have too much and disown you and say, 'Who is the Lord?' Or I may become poor and steal, and so dishonor the name of my God."[21] This is one of my favorite verses in scripture because it helps me find a balance between greed and economic insufficiency. Although I have always been comfortable economically, I have also been greedy and fully recognize that "Dear God, please don't give me riches" is not a very American prayer. *The Prayer of Jabez* sold 20 million copies by promising wealth to Christians who prayed this way: "Oh, that you would bless me and enlarge my border."[22] It was all about getting more, all about *not* being content. But "don't give me poverty" is an understandable human prayer no matter where you are. This proverb is a lens into the better and the worse, the genius and the stupidity, of the prosperity message.

Carlos Alberto, the millionaire pastor of the billion-dollar Universal Church of God's Kingdom in Brazil, says he preaches prosperity because "when you have someone in the audience with four hungry children, it's hard to tell them to wait for their reward in the next life."[23] He is absolutely right, and his explanation shows why the prosperity message is grounded in truth—God is indeed concerned for those four children and wants them to be fed. As a Pentecostal theologian, I will go so far as to say that God hates poverty, defined as "the state of having little or no money and few or no material possessions" along with "a lack of opportunity and empowerment, and bad quality of life in general."[24] Not being able to feed your family or send your child to first grade is deplorable, and that's the situation of half the population of the globe. This is understood well by Latino immigrants in America, as Arlene Sanchez Walsh notes: "The pastors view their theology as one of liberation: *God wants to heal you. God wants you to prosper. You don't have to wait. You don't have to be tied down by your immigrant circumstances.* It is a powerful message to immigrant and assimilated Latinos alike, since both score lower than whites on a whole scale of measurables: education, finances, health care, etc."[25] Praying to God for an end to poverty, having faith it's going to end, and working for a brighter tomorrow are all good. And in most countries in the world, Pentecostals are significantly more likely than other Christians to believe that their future financial prospects are bright.[26]

The prosperity teaching is at least going in the right direction, toward recognition that God despises poverty. I would argue that God also wants Pentecostals to see and help change the business and political realities that perpetuate poverty. Feeding a homeless person is great, but getting the U.S. government to allocate more funding for low-income housing actually helps alleviate homelessness. Maybe the televangelists could raise money for free health clinics, low-income housing, job training, and lobbying their governments to address social ills.

In fact, the large majority of Pentecostals believe that they should be politically engaged and active. A greater percentage of Pentecostals believe this than average citizens. Imagine the potential if the wisdom of the prosperity message, tempered to be more biblical by being less focused on individual greed and wealth accumulation, could be focused on the policies that would bring true prosperity to millions more folks who need it. Something like "We Pentecostals know God is against poverty and is for prosperity, and we encourage the government to reallocate more money for education and health care."

It is similar to theological arguments against racism or sexism that are based in our understanding of what heaven will be like—all ethnicities will be there, and we won't hate each other in heaven, so we can and should get along now in light of the fact that we'll be spending eternity together. The church can embrace the end of all things now. Men won't be sexist in heaven, so why be sexist now? God's ultimate plan is for reconciliation and unity, and the church can reveal that now to the world. In the same way, prosperity teaching sees that people will not be starving and barely subsisting in heaven. In heaven, ten-year-old Indian children will not be working sixteen-hour days to produce clothing for Americans.[27] There will be no sweatshops in heaven. But there is poverty and extreme suffering now. Prosperity preachers have tapped into a truth about God's concern for human financial and physical needs, but it has gone to the extreme, perhaps because the church has for too long ignored the holistic gospel of Jesus Christ.

If we look at the world of money and financial resources like a mountain with a really wide base and a tiny snow-covered peak, we can see both the promise and the peril of prosperity teaching and why there is so much wisdom in "neither poverty nor riches." To those who make up the base of the mountain—three billion people, or half the population of the world—moving from $1 per day to $2 per day to $3 per day is being delivered from the oppression of poverty. They're not becoming rich; they're simply escaping poverty. They can care for their families better, send their children to elementary school, visit a health clinic and buy penicillin, perhaps even have furniture. That is a godly message of deliverance and hope. Luke tells us that when Jesus taught his disciples what is often called the Sermon on the Mount, "he went down with them and stood on a level place."[28] This is why some scholars call Luke's version the Sermon on the Plain. From this level place on the side of the mountain, Jesus encouraged the poor, hungry, and weeping ones and said they would be satisfied and comforted. Jesus criticized the rich, well-fed, laughing ones and said they would weep. Jesus' message is good news to all, even the rich and well fed, but we often don't receive it that way even though we can.

But Jesus' message is especially good news to the poor who have hope that they can travel up the mountain a little and have enough. The good news of Jesus is deliverance from both poverty and riches—for both are burdens that make the world a worse place. I can see Jesus looking down the mountain and welcoming the poor and downtrodden, and he looks up the mountain and welcomes the rich and affluent to give generously and quit hoarding. There is a level place on the side of the mountain where there is enough for all.

The prosperity gospel sounds absurd to those of us at the peak, who consume almost 90 percent of the world's resources—we are the wealthy and prosperous ones. The prosperity gospel can appeal to the wealthy only if we are greedy, if we want to be even higher up the mountain, to be at the pinnacle and look down on as much of the rest of humanity as possible. But the prosperity gospel appeals to those at the bottom of the mountain in what I consider to be healthy ways. Poor folk can be greedy as well, but hoping to escape squalor is not greed; it's a more than legitimate response to the invitation to move up the mountain, an invitation straight from the heart of God.

It seems to me that the prosperity message has emerged for several good reasons. It is a corrective to the overly spiritual, body- and earth-denying focus on the soul of many kinds of Christianity. Christians have famously tried to save "souls" but have often forgotten or ignored the fact that God is concerned for the whole person. The Assemblies of God statement against prosperity teaching is dangerously complicit in this overly spiritual focus, claiming that adherents of "name it and claim it" faith teaching can be "more concerned with physical and material prosperity than with spiritual growth."[29] This assumes that spiritual growth is independent from and more important than physical and material well-being. But it's not, and prosperity theology unites them. Prosperity theology properly recognizes that this world matters and that God wants to lift people out of their despair in the here and now. The Pentecostal prosperity gospel challenges the idea that Christianity is just about heaven or life after death or "the sweet bye-and-bye." It brings the promise and hope of healthy life with God to the present.

Mary, mother of Jesus, said in Luke 1:53 that God wants to fill the hungry with good things. There is no need to "spiritualize" this—feeding the hungry is spiritual, and it is what God wants. The Law given to Moses said that there should be "no needy among you" because government and the community of the faithful will be wise and generous with the resources of creation. Economic sufficiency characterized the plan for the world because God wants people and creation not just to survive but to thrive. The prosperity message claims that poverty is an insult to God and can be overcome. Acts 2, 4, and 6 show this possibility because the generosity of the early Christians meant "there were no needy among them." Christian silence about unjust policies that allow a few to get rich at the expense of millions (or billions) creates an atmosphere where the Christian promise of prosperity is justifiably desirable. The prosperity gospel took one very inaccurate, unbalanced, and tortuous Christian teaching—God is concerned only about your spirit or soul—and reacted with another extreme—God wants you to be as wealthy as Bill Gates.

The economic contexts of Latin America, Africa, and Asia have been dismal for decades. Prosperity theology churches exploded in Brazil in the 1980s and 1990s during times of terrible unemployment, excessive inflation, and political instability.

During the same time, Nigeria experienced a 1,000 percent devaluation of its currency, and real income per person dropped 90 percent in only eight years (1985–1993).[30] People in two-thirds of the world were feeling the consequences of globalization and urbanization. For those with no job and no prospects, the message that God can miraculously turn one's finances around is obviously appealing. And prosperity churches sometimes include education about financial stewardship along with their messages of tithing to receive a hundredfold return. One prosperity pastor in Nigeria encouraged the women in his congregation to invest in chickens and increase the size of their flocks rather than eat them.[31] So the women developed small businesses that benefited their extended families. One Pentecostal physician in Ethiopia opened health clinics in her city's slums, and some churches even provide microenterprise loans, job training, and affordable housing. Other Pentecostals advocate for a living wage and provide tuition assistance to members.[32]

According to Luke, Jesus preached his first hometown sermon on this passage from Isaiah: "The Spirit of the Lord is upon me, because he has anointed me to preach good news to the poor . . . to release the oppressed, to proclaim Jubilee year!" Jubilee year is a biblical practice of forgiving debts, returning land to its original owner, and freeing slaves. Jesus said it was time to relieve people of financial debts. According to Luke, Jesus' followers took him seriously; they shared their money and resources and cared for one another economically, and "there were no needy persons among them."[33]

Americans owe $2.55 trillion in consumer debt, $962 billion of which is on credit cards at an average interest rate of 18.9 percent.[34] That's an average of more than $8,000 per household.[35] The odds are that you yourself have debt that is not a mortgage or a car; I certainly do.

Carl and Janice Beaver, members of Mount Carmel Missionary Church in Norfolk, Virginia, owed $10,500 in credit card debt when they went to church one night. Little did they know, or expect, that when they left a couple of hours later, they would be debt-free. But they were. For their pastor had received a Jubilee vision based on Acts 2, and his monthly "debt liquidation revivals" had already paid off over $300,000 worth of members' credit card debt. The Beavers were debt-free family number 56, and they went home "shoutin' glory!"[36]

So what do Jesus, the Pentecostal prosperity gospel, and painful American consumer debt have in common? Mount Carmel's pastor, Bishop Vernie Russell, had realized that members of his church, like most Americans, struggle with debt and financial insecurity. So he started teaching financial planning and encouraged people to shred their credit cards. He even started collecting the cut-up cards in a large glass bowl at the front of the auditorium as a testimony to the deliverance and freedom that comes from such a significant lifestyle change. He developed a "Declaration of Financial Empowerment," and his church members pledged:

- To save and invest 10 to 15 percent of my after-tax income
- To be a proactive and informed investor
- To be a disciplined and knowledgeable consumer
- To engage in sound budget, credit, and tax management practices
- To teach business and financial principles to my children
- To use a portion of my personal wealth to strengthen my community[37]

One woman started a sewing business; many parishioners increased the amounts they paid toward their debts and focused on their smaller bills first so they could see their progress. But Bishop Russell also realized that in Acts the people actually shared their money and that this empowered them even more. He noted that in his church, "a lot of people were hurting, but they hadn't complained and nobody was aware."[38] Some were even in danger of bankruptcy and about to lose their homes. After reading Acts 2:42–47, one of the most important chapters in the Bible for Pentecostals, he announced that he felt the Spirit leading his church members to work together to pay off their credit card debts.

> Everyone was filled with awe, and many wonders and miraculous signs were done by the apostles. All the believers were together and had everything in common. They sold their possessions and goods as anyone had need and gave them what they needed. . . . And the Lord added to their number daily those who were being saved. . . . No one claimed that any of his possessions was his own, but they shared everything they had. . . . There were no needy persons among them.[39]

Bishop Russell preaches that "you can't serve both MasterCard and the Master," but he testifies that the hardest service was the first one because nobody had seen it work. Nevertheless, they raised $5,600 that first day and paid off one family's debt. The family brought its bills to the pastor and trustees, who then sent a check directly to the creditor. Every three months, all of the debt-free families attend a seminar on staying solvent, and they are encouraged to contribute each month toward paying off the next family's debt. The pastor teaches that they should not make any major purchases for seven months, and when they finally do, items should be bought with cash rather than credit. So far, there have been no "backsliders," for not a single family has gone back into debt, and members haven't left the church after getting their debts paid off. Why would you want to leave a community full of people who take care of each other like that? The church is growing, and tithes were up 25 percent in the first year that Bishop Russell started his debt liquidation revivals.

These Friday nights of Pentecostal rejoicing and sharing are filled with floor-thumping music and Spirit-filled dancing.

A *Wall Street Journal* reporter noted that the congregation chanted and sang, "The devil is defeated, he is defeated. . . . Stomp, stomp, stomp on the devil!"[40] This church recognizes the crushing and demonic pain of real economic debt, just like the Bible emphasizes. They are healing the unbiblical and dangerous spiritualizing of the debt passages in scripture, such as "forgive us our debts as we forgive our debtors." That is not just talking about sin; it is talking about financial debt, and Bishop Russell knows it. God *is* concerned about money, about dollars, about debt, and about bank accounts. Bishop Russell says, "The credit card companies don't like me too well."[41] He's doing something that is truly led by the Holy Spirit, for those who rejoice are those being delivered, and those who are grumbling are those who were gorging themselves on other people's suffering. Perhaps this is one way the Pentecostal message of prosperity can be embodied, in ways that are uplifting but not greedy, ways that leave people neither in the valley nor at the peak but bring us together at the level place on the side of the mountain.

CHAPTER 5

STORYTELLING

There may be no two things more powerful in
human communication than storytelling and music.

—*Tex Sample*

The other day, I was at a church that had a "testimony service." Anyone who had something to share with the congregation, whether good or bad, happy or sad, could stand up and tell his or her story. The church family of about two hundred people took the time to hear the burdens and joys of lives in our very midst.

A young woman in her early twenties stood first and shared that her father had gone to South Africa on a mission trip, had suddenly fallen ill, and was rapidly deteriorating. She requested prayer for him and for her mother and the rest of the family who were so worried. She also asked for wisdom that the people there would know how best to care for him and show their love since he was so far away from home.

A young husband and wife stood next. He put his arm around her and held her close; they smiled out at the congregation and announced, "We're going to have a baby." We all erupted into applause. Then there was a family who had been trying to adopt for quite some time. They received word that week that they had been chosen by a fifteen-year-old who was due in only three weeks! They asked for prayer and wisdom for the mother and sixteen-year-old father, their families, and the baby. They also didn't want to get their hopes up because it might not work out. So they rejoiced and also asked for prayer for themselves, especially their biological nine-year-old daughter, who *was* hopeful.

Next a thirty-something woman asked for prayer for her sister, who was entering a drug and alcohol abuse rehabilitation program. Her sister had been in and out of rehab before, so she needed prayer that it would actually help her this time. The lady asking for prayer also wanted to be less skeptical and more open to her sister's ability to change. Another woman who had been out of work for a while stood to ask for prayer for an upcoming job interview that she was excited about.

Then a woman asked forgiveness from the congregation for not living like Jesus in her business situation. She confessed that she'd been too cynical toward her employers and had participated in gossip and backbiting. She wanted to do better and be the light she knew she was called to be at work, so she asked for forgiveness and prayer. A father reported that his youngest son's surgery went well. Finally, Joanne shared that she would be having a double mastectomy because of cancer in one breast and the high chances that it would spread. She hadn't had a mammogram in five years and is thankful that on a whim she went in and the cancer was caught early. She told us that she had a rare hereditary mutation, so she needed a full mastectomy, and that she was angry and anxious and wanted to be in a better place before she went in for the surgery. She also grinned and asked that we pray that the physicians would have a stellar day and bring their "A" game when they operated on her.

In Pentecostal churches around the world, our personal stories matter enough to share, and all of our stories interweave at church. Not just before and after, but during the service, in the middle of the liturgy, in the work of worship, there is time for storytelling. We are served by hearing one another's stories, and we serve God by rejoicing with those who rejoice and weeping with those who weep. We don't just tell and hear the stories of Jesus and the Bible or listen to the stories of the pastor or preacher; we tell our own and hear those of our friends.

The Bible Is Mostly Stories, or, Once Upon a Time Jesus Told a Lot of Stories

Christians live in an ancient narrative, some of which goes like this. Around four thousand years ago, God called Abraham and Sarah out of southern Iraq; they left family and friends to follow as faithfully as they could to Palestine. Abraham almost killed his second-born son Isaac on an altar of stones when God asked him to; the gods Abraham was familiar with asked for human sacrifice, so this new God did not seem that different. But this new God was very different and said that human sacrifices weren't necessary after all; animals would be fine for now. So Isaac survived the near-disembowelment, and he and his wife, Rebekah, had twins. Jacob, the younger twin, was a liar whose name (which meant "liar") was changed to Israel after he wrestled with God. Israel and his harem (two wives and two other women who produced children for him) had twelve sons and one daughter, Dinah. When a neighbor raped Dinah, Israel's sons deceived and murdered all the men in the neighbor's village and took all the children and women as plunder.

Later, most of Israel's sons got angry at their brother Joseph, the next to youngest, and sold him to human traffickers headed to Egypt to sell slaves. Joseph found himself a slave of Potiphar, one of the highest-ranking political leaders of Egypt. But Potiphar's wife accused Joseph of attempted rape, so Joseph was put in the dungeon to die a slow, tormented death. While there, he interpreted the nightmares and dreams of other prisoners. Eventually, a released convict remembered him, and Joseph interpreted a dream for Pharaoh himself. Joseph then became second-in-command of Egypt, saved it from starvation when a drought came, married an African woman, and reconciled with his family.

But within a few years, this family of immigrants from Iraq and Palestine were enslaved by the Egyptians. Four hundred years later, their family had grown so much that the pharaoh, in fear, ordered genocidal infanticide—he wanted all the baby boys of these Hebrews ("wanderers") killed. But one mother risked the lives of her family by committing civil disobedience: she put her baby in the crocodile-infested river inside a protective basket. Pharaoh's daughter found the baby, Moses, so he ended up in the king's house. Moses then got a world-class education but knew he was actually from the immigrant laboring class; he eventually murdered one of the Egyptian slave masters for beating down a Hebrew slave. Moses ran for his life and lived in the desert, married an African woman named Zipporah, and tended sheep. But God called him back to Egypt to persuade his politically powerful adopted family to free his economically disenfranchised blood family.

The rapes, murders, slavery, torture, wars, poverty, faithlessness, reconciliations, love, hope, perseverance, community building, strength, forgiveness, and faithfulness continue all the way through the Hebrew scriptures (Old Testament) and the Christian scriptures (New Testament). Women drive tent pegs through the heads of sleeping generals (Judges 4–5). A widowed daughter-in-law exposes injustice by disguising herself as a prostitute and having sex with her hypocritical father-in-law, whom she later rightly humiliates in public when he tries to have her executed for getting pregnant without being married (Genesis 38). A tortured carpenter forgives the religious elites and foreign invaders *while* they are murdering him (Luke 23:34). A religious extremist who assassinates and imprisons both women and men for God lays down his sword, apologizes, is transformed, and is then hunted down by his former allies (Acts). Prophets tell kings they are greedy and being mean to poor people; kings kill prophets (Amos, Isaiah).

The Bible is mostly stories, character-forming stories, and for Christians, the stories of Jesus and his followers are supposed to be the central ones. We are "formed by stories we did not create,"[1] and the story of our lives finds meaning in the stories we tell from the Bible and the way we narrate our own lives. We could justify our massacre of a city in retaliation for an attack by telling certain stories from the Bible, or we could forgive our enemies based on other stories in the same Bible. How we tell those stories will determine how *our* stories go. Pentecostals tell the stories of signs, wonders, and miracles, and that's what their stories are about.

Stanley Hauerwas, declared America's best theologian by *Time* magazine, says that stories are the most fundamental way to talk of God.[2] Stories are not illustrations of deeper truths; stories *are* the deeper truths. We learn about God, about ourselves, and about the world through stories. Rather than ask for the point of the story, we live the stories, for "the narratives are the point." We get to know each other by telling our stories; after hearing the life story of a new friend, you wouldn't dare ask, "So what's the point?" Pentecostals live in and tell the biblical stories and "gratefully inherit a tradition"[3] of signs and wonders, miracles, spiritual warfare, prayers, prophecy, God's closeness, and Spirit empowerment. Their storytelling—the miracles, the healings, the sufferings, the successes—shapes their world and creates a world in which they can live. As Hauerwas says, "We can only act within the world [story] we can envision."[4]

Pentecostals as storytellers create and envision worlds of transformation, hope, and wonder that people can live in. Stories give us our sense of self and help us move from our past to our future, toward the purpose of our lives.[5] The Pentecostal story is that God is active in this world and that we can be a part of God's miraculous and prophetic work. As Hauerwas says:

> The church is the lively argument, extended over centuries and occasioned by the stories of God's calling of Israel and of the life and death of Jesus Christ, to which we are invited to contribute by learning to live faithful to those stories. It is the astounding

claim of Christians that through this particular man's story, we discover our true selves and thus are made part of God's very life. We
become part of God's story by finding our lives within that story.[6]

Jesus is a story, and the story of Jesus is full of stories
Jesus told. To be a Christian is to learn to grow into the story
of Jesus and his followers.[7] For example, there is a great story of
how the religious elites rejected Jesus because he ate and drank
with outcasts, but these despised outcasts loved Jesus. This confused John the Baptist and his followers; they weren't quite sure
if Jesus was really the Messiah. So John sent his friends to ask
Jesus, "Are you really the one? Or should we expect someone
else?" Jesus responded by complimenting John's prophetic life of
simplicity: "Is he a man dressed in fine clothes? No, those who
wear expensive clothes and indulge in luxury are in palaces.
But who is John? A prophet? Yes, and more than a prophet!" But
then Jesus poked fun at the self-important religious leaders who
rejected both John and Jesus, and he highlighted the way he and
his followers are supposed to live in the world. "For John the
Baptist came neither eating bread nor drinking wine, and you say
'He has a demon.' The Son of Man came eating and drinking,
and you say, 'Here is a glutton and a drunkard, a friend of tax
collectors and 'sinners.'" Learning to live in the story of Jesus, as
a follower of Jesus, means learning to live so that your enemies
can accuse you of being a drunken friend of sinners. Then, like
Jesus, you respond, "Wisdom is proved right by all her children."[8]

Pentecostals have a particular way of growing into the story
of Jesus that connects their lives to the specific lives of Jesus
and his followers—they tell Jesus stories and Jesus follower stories and quote what Jesus said to his disciples: "You are going
to be able to do even greater works than these!"[9] The book of
Acts in the New Testament is the story of the greater works that
Jesus' followers did, and Acts has only twenty-eight chapters.
But Pentecostals would be glad to be acknowledged as the next
chapter of the same story. It is central to their identity to be that

story; in fact, if something is in Acts, Pentecostals are looking for it to be a part of their own experience, too. The best way to show the story-formed nature of "even greater works than these" is to tell you a Pentecostal story.

Pentecostalism as Acts 29: The Story Continues

Right before my senior year in college, I spent a summer in Mexico with other Pentecostal college students, helping to get a new church started. We put up a big yellow-and-white tent on a vacant lot and spent a portion of each day inviting people to our *campaña de fe* (campaign of faith), which we held every night for six weeks. As we visited homes in the surrounding neighborhoods, we would play soccer and basketball with the kids, hand out *bolantes* (flyers), and pray for people who wanted prayer. We spent a lot of time memorizing scripture as well— especially the stories about healing and miracles. Dr. Jefferson (not his real name), a former longtime missionary who was now our professor and leader, had us locate, number, and memorize every scripture passage or verse that contained a miracle or healing in the books of Mark, Luke, and Acts. My Bible still has those numbers in it; I used blue ink in Mark and Luke and black ink in Acts. As a twenty-year-old cross-cultural missions major in Nuevas Casas Grandes, Mexico, I found twenty-one such passages in Mark, twenty-six in Luke, and nineteen in Acts.

Dr. Jefferson's exercise of having us find the miracle stories in the Bible was intentionally and explicitly supposed to have us connect our experiences and expectations with the biblical narrative. At our first daily devotion, this is what we heard: "God wants to heal everybody. Jesus always heals, teaches, and preaches. . . . There will be many more gradual healings than instantaneous ones. . . . All the sick are not going to be healed, but Christ wants to heal all. We want the news of the healings to spread around."[10] He told us a story of a blind man who had two empty sockets when he started attending a previous faith campaign, but two months later he had two eyeballs—even though he got only one at a time! The blind man did not get his eyeballs through implants or any medical treatment; it was a flat-out miracle. Although I had never kept a journal before, I decided to keep one during my summer in Mexico precisely because I thought amazing things would be happening as we lived as continuations of the stories in Acts.

At the first evening service, four people were healed, including a blind man who received sight and a girl cured of appendicitis. At the second service, five were healed, and at the third service, another man with poor vision was healed—and Dr. Jefferson tested him by having him walk to the back of the tent and say how many fingers the man could see him holding up. The elderly man, who said his vision had been blurry for many years, passed with flying colors. The people healed nightly ranged from as few as none to as many as five over the course of the six weeks of services. One man, healed of deafness, asked for the microphone and told the audience that when he was young, he had seen a man dead for seventy-two hours raised to life.

Our lives during this time were focused on being the biblical people, no holds barred. One afternoon, one of the students said this clearly in her Acts 9:32–35 Bible study for us: "Peter traveled about the country, and we are traveling around just like him. We can live by the same boldness, and Christ can work through us in the same way. Peter 'found a man' and prayed for him, and we will find people as we go around. Jesus heals, Peter knew who the healer was, and we know who the healer is too."[11] Later that day, my friend Marco and I prayed for a man who had only one eye; I recorded in my journal that "we could see the skin move under the lid like an eyeball was in there. I'm gonna keep praying for him." A little while later, some of the girls in our group went to the home of a little girl who could not speak. The parents wanted them to pray for their "mute" girl, and after they did, the little girl asked for a tortilla.

A few days later, after another discipleship class focusing on the biblical stories of healing (this particular devotion included nine different stories), I had the following experience:

We went out at 11:00 A.M. to go house-to-house and get to know people. The first house we went in, a man had fallen and broken both legs and had to have an operation, but he hadn't walked for six years. He was in a wheelchair. I quoted scripture to him, and he wanted us to pray. I held his hand and we prayed. He gripped my hand so hard and wouldn't let go. We prayed and then gave them a Gospel of John. Junia led them through it, and they said they'd like us to come back tomorrow. We will. The next house I felt definitely led to. There was a lady that came to the door. When I saw her (Francisca), I felt the Spirit lead me to ask if she had any needs she'd like us to pray for. I could sense her pain in her eyes. She asked us in and told us she had diabetes, bad kidneys, and high blood pressure. I quoted 1 John 5:14 (confidence in approaching God) and "by his stripes we are healed" and "he sent forth His word and healed them." I said if she believed in Jesus, He would heal her. I have been praying for compassion and we went to her to pray and I just started weeping and we prayed. I felt God's special presence like I never had. He was there. When we were done, I felt like I should ask her if she felt better. I asked her to be honest. When she looked up, her pain and burden were gone! She said that she felt a warmth go all through her feet up through her body. We all *knew* she had been healed. She said there was no pain. I told her she had received her healing and she just needed to believe and continue to claim her healing. She said she would come to the campaign. She wants us to come back tomorrow. God really was good; He is increasing my faith as I exercise it. It won't grow unless I use it.[12]

Our daily intake of healing stories from the Bible and healing stories from our experiences created an atmosphere in which we really did feel like we were a continuation of the biblical story; we *were* Acts 29. Over the course of our six weeks in Mexico,

I recorded that we saw a total of thirty-five healings, a little less than one per day. But the emphasis here is not on the signs and wonders themselves; it's on the storied reality in which they flow. There is little abstract argumentation for the reality of the possibility of signs and wonders; there are a lot of stories from scripture and experience to situate the expectation in our very own daily lives.

On July 2, I recorded that Dr. Jefferson said, "Every Christian can pray for the sick and see them healed. Give God the opportunity." The next afternoon, Samantha, one of the students, led the devotion and told the story of Tabitha being raised from the dead (Acts 9:36–42). She noted that even though the family called for *Peter* to pray for Tabitha, "the promise is for everyone." Later that day, some ladies came to our home.

> One had problems with demons in her house—so after lunch we drove over there and drove out the demons. It was a glorious time of exercising our authority over Stupid [our nickname for the devil] in the name of Jesus! Discipleship class was at 4:30 since we exorcised some demons. After class we went and played basketball. The guys were very friendly, and I led one through some of the San Juan [Gospel of Saint John]. We gave them some tracts and *bolantes*—hopefully they'll come to the campaign tonight.[13]

Telling the biblical stories and becoming the story means that Pentecostals nonchalantly weave together exorcisms and basketball in a way that's as natural as taters and gravy or beans and rice.

Witches, Wizards, and Christ, Oh My!
The Power of Conversion Stories

In the next chapter, we'll explore why Pentecostalism's approach to power and spiritual warfare is so appealing in much of the world, but stories about conversion from the dark side also spark imagination and fuel growth.

Some of those stories are fake, like Mike Warnke's fabricated history of being a high priest in Satanism. He claimed that before converting to Christianity, he led a coven of fifteen hundred witches and wizards who performed human sacrifices and other grisly practices. He then built a twenty-year career telling his testimony as a quite entertaining "Christian comedian," making as much as $2 million annually, before being debunked in 1992 by a Christian magazine.[14] Some analysts think that *The Satan Seller*, the popular book that told his conversion story, was almost singlehandedly responsible for the Satanism scare of the 1980s in the United States.[15]

As a teenager, I attended one of Warnke's concerts in Tulsa, Oklahoma, at the height of his popularity and thought it was pretty cool that we were able to afford one of his comedy albums. I enjoyed listening to it and learned all about the reality of Satanism in America, at least the reality according to Mike Warnke. I was shocked and a little disappointed a few years later when I found out he was a fraud, but that revelation didn't yet change my understanding of the occult.

But there are plenty of real wizards, shamans, and "witch doctors" who do convert to Pentecostal Christianity in Africa and Asia. Rather than an uncorroborated story like Warnke's, these conversions are of well-known witch doctors who use all manner of items to cast spells, charms, and curses. Bok-hee Lim, a Korean shaman who strongly opposed Christianity, became a follower of Jesus after Pentecostals repeatedly walked around her neighborhood praying for her and their other neighbors. Bok-hee then destroyed the temple to her god that she had built in her backyard, burned five car trunks full of clothes and paraphernalia that she used in her shamanism practice, and testified, "Because it was a confrontation between a demigod and the almighty God, the demigod could do nothing but . . . be defeated in a groggy state without even having a real fight."[16] The neighbors all watched this happen; they knew Bok-hee was a shaman, and many had paid for her services and watched her work for years.

When well-established anti-Christian folks who work for the enemy change sides, those are stories worth trumpeting; it's the religious version of a passionate Republican becoming an enthusiastic Democrat (or vice versa). Can you imagine the testimony of someone like Rush Limbaugh converting to the Democratic party and telling the story of how wrong he had been and how he now sees the light? Those kinds of conversions embolden the folks who receive them and weaken and raise questions among those who lose one of their committed advocates. In fact, the conversion of witch doctors in Africa and Asia are often followed by entire villages becoming Christian. Kefa Sempangi tells of a prominent Ugandan witch doctor who burned all her magical tools, an act that "initiated a mass conversion among local magicians."[17] These stories are told and retold in oral cultures, on the radio, and on television and become very popular pamphlets, articles, and books. One scholar notes that these stories are a thriving genre of religious popular culture.[18]

In fact, it reminds us of the great conversion story of Saul, the one who killed Christians in the name of his god. Saul watched and approved as his friends used jagged rocks to torture and murder Stephen. He traveled for miles looking for Christians so he could drag them to prison and have them executed. But Saul saw the light of Jesus, the scales fell from his eyes, and he became Paul the Apostle.[19] Saint Paul's story and his ministry that followed shaped the future of Christianity, and the stories and ministries of the witch doctor converts in Africa and Asia are shaping Christianity now.

What's the Appeal?

Joel Osteen, the pastor of a humongous Charismatic church in Houston, Texas, starts each sermon with a short "kinda funny" story like this one: "I heard about these two little boys, they were spending the night with their grandparents. Before they went to bed they got down on their knees to say their prayers. The youngest one started praying at the top of his lungs, 'God, I PRAY you'll give me A NEW BICYCLE. And I PRAY you'll give me A NEW PLAYSTATION. And I PRAY you'll give me A NEW DVD PLAYER.' His brother said, 'Why are you scream-ing? God is not deaf.' The little boy said, 'I know that, but grandmother is.'"[20] Whether you like the joke or not, it leads well into the typical way that Pentecostals preach—with lots of stories. Stories of danger, disease, and death that often turn into stories of healing, hope, and happiness.

The great appeal of stories can be seen in the fact that the American and European movie and television industries (which almost exclusively tell stories) generate hundreds of billions of dollars in income annually.[21] The average American watches more than four hours of television a day—that's two solid months a year, or nine years of a person's life (if you live to be sixty-five).[22] Americans rent six million DVDs each day, and together we watch 250 billion hours of television each year. We really like stories, and we're willing to devote much of our lives and money to hearing and seeing them. The rest of the world also loves stories—India produces almost one thousand movies per year (50 percent more than the United States).[23]

I had almost finished writing this chapter on stories and sto-rytelling when I read *Made to Stick: Why Some Ideas Survive and Others Die*.[24] In it, a couple of brothers, one a professor of organi-zational behavior at Stanford and the other a former researcher at Harvard, analyze what makes ideas "sticky," that is, interest-ing and easy to remember. It turns out that telling and hearing stories are key ingredients in sticky ideas. And sticky ideas cre-ate sticky movements—movements that people are attracted to and that keep on growing. Much research has been done on the power of stories, and it consistently points to a powerful reason why Pentecostalism is so amazingly appealing—it's a storytelling and story-living religion that produces *action*.

Stories contain wisdom and are effective teaching tools; they also can inspire people and compel us to action. You could tell someone that there are two billion people living in poverty in our world, but the odds are you will not get them to write a check to help feed children by citing that statistic.[25] Instead, you could tell this true story of Elosy, who lives in Meru, Kenya:

> After losing both parents to . . . AIDS . . . , Elosy, who was just 10, was left with her crippled grandmother Rael . . . who only has one leg and is very poor. She can't work on her small farm because of her handicap, and getting food for Elosy was difficult. Through helpful Christian people in the area, Elosy's grandmother got some food and clothing, but the young girl sometimes had to beg for help. Her grandmother wanted Elosy to go to school but could not regularly afford the expenses. . . . Elosy confesses that she didn't have decent clothing, bedding, or food. She often felt lonely, especially when the other children would tease her about both her parents dying of AIDS and her grandmother being a crippled older woman living in poverty. . . . Today, Elosy is happy and living in a Pentecostal children's home. She has friends to play with . . . in an environment where she is not teased. . . . She is able to attend school regularly and feels equal with other children. She works for a better life to help her grandmother and others who are less fortunate.[26]

According to most research, the right stories help people act. They provide knowledge about the world and motivation to live and act in certain ways. Even more amazingly, the listeners of a story often mingle their own lives with the protagonist in the story being told. There is no such thing as a passive audience when stories are being told. In other words, listening to a story activates our brains as if we were doing the actions ourselves—our brains are preparing us to perform the very actions we are hearing about in the stories. As the scientists say, "Being the audience isn't so passive after all. Inside, we're getting ready to act."[27]

This is all well illustrated by my mission trip to Mexico. First, every day we read stories from the Bible in which followers of Jesus came across sick people and prayed for them, and they were healed. Second, we heard stories of other people's experiences, times when they prayed for people who were eventually healed (like Dr. Jefferson praying for the man without eyeballs). Third, we told the biblical and regular-life stories each night to the people who came to the *campaña de fe*. Fourth, we took action on these stories and did the same things ourselves—praying for sick people and believing that the same things could happen. Our personal stories merged with the biblical stories and the stories of those around us; we were shaped by the stories we read and heard.

To Pentecostal Christians in Pune, India (or anywhere else in the world), telling a story from the book of Acts in which Peter reaches out and heals someone prepares them to do the same thing in the twenty-first century. Pentecostal stories of conversion, success, and deliverance invite others to imagine their lives of conversion, success, and deliverance. When Joel Osteen starts with a "kinda funny" story about a boy praying for a new bicycle, he is opening up his audience for more inspirational or challenging stories that always follow. These stories warn against harmful actions, like how my cousin Bob ended up in prison again because he would not stop using drugs, even though his uncle had given him a good job and his mother and father were trying to help. They can also inspire, as when my friends Andy and Sara decided to eat out a little less and give a little more to the orphanage in Meru, Kenya, so that now Jediel and Felicity are receiving an education and have a home with Elosy.

Just like the biblical stories, our stories are a mixture of both grief and rejoicing. Remember the testimony and prayer request service I was at recently? The family that was cautiously excited about adopting a baby in just three weeks had to make a radical adjustment when the fifteen-year-old birth mother changed her mind and decided to keep her daughter the day after she was born (although they were able to adopt a different newborn baby girl a few months later), and the girl's father who got sick while in Africa passed away three days later. But Joanne's double mastectomy went perfectly, and no cancer was found at all.

Although the telling of stories can be gimmicky, poorly done, and abused, it can also be authentic and life-changing. Stories communicate the truth of the gospel and the truth of our real lives. Stories open up new vistas for us to live in and open our eyes to new possibilities. If you can go to church and hear interesting stories that connect with your real life and if the life you live during the week is empowered and helped because of the stories you heard at church, why wouldn't you want to go to that church? In fact, if something happens in your own personal story that you think is worth sharing, you get to tell people who intentionally create space for you to do so.

CHAPTER 6

POWER AND SPIRITUAL WARFARE

If Satan troubles us, Jesus Christ,
You are the lion of the grasslands.
Your claws are sharp.
You will tear out his entrails and
Leave them on the ground for the flies to eat.
                —*Afua Kuma, West African Pentecostal pastor*

Resist the devil, and he will flee from you.
                                        —*James 4:7*

Have you ever seen a ghost, spirit, or apparition in real life? My friend Dawn, a born and bred Pentecostal, has seen between six and ten each year since she was twenty-two years old. Here is a report of one of her experiences with her husband, Chris.

Chris and I were at a Christian retreat at a conference center. I woke up in the middle of the night to see a lady pacing in our room. She was a heavyset lady, with long dark hair and a long dark white robe, and she was barefoot. We were in a bunk bed, and our daughter, Lauren, was in a Pack 'n Play on the other side of the room. The lady was pacing the room between us and Lauren. I didn't speak with her, though; I could just feel her in my mind and communicate with her that way. I watched her for a little bit, and she turned around and just stared at me, not as a standoff, just looking at me. I was thinking, "What are you doing here?" She seemed like she could have been thinking exactly the same thing, she was so comfortably pacing back and forth in our room. Finally, I decided I wanted to go back to sleep and was uncomfortable with her being between Lauren and me. I was really just more tired of it than freaked out; it's hard to go to sleep when a stranger is there.

So in my mind I said, "OK, you need to go." And she looked at me kind of sadly and then paced a little more. I wasn't freaked out and I wasn't scared. I had always been told that you have to use the name of Jesus to tell spirits what to do, and I had told her once and she didn't leave and just looked sad. So in my head again I said, "In Jesus' name, you need to go." She stopped and looked at me again, shrugged her shoulders, walked down by the end of the bunk bed, stopped for a second, and looked back at me again, kind of sad and defeated. I mentally said it again nicely: "In Jesus' name, you need to go." She left looking sad. I didn't mention it to Chris that night or the next day; such events were common enough in my life for me not to mention this one.[1]

Dawn doesn't ever get the feeling that these spirits are bad. She says they just seem neutral, neither good nor bad. This could fit with some African and Asian worldviews that hold that the recently dead are still with us, should be cared for, and can be contacted. In fact, they see death as only a physical separation, not destruction, and deceased family members can even reveal themselves to others when they wish.

I attended a Pentecostal seminary to work on a master of divinity degree so that I could become a missionary to the Middle East. I took as many classes as I could that focused on Muslim culture, and one professor that I really enjoyed was Dr. Sobhi Malek, an Egyptian Muslim who had converted to Pentecostal Christianity. Probably only Pentecostals offer courses in accredited seminaries titled "Power Encounter," and that's the class where I heard this story:

Dr. Malek was visiting a friend of his who was a city official in Egypt. They were sitting in the living room talking, and his friend asked if he would like something to drink, perhaps a soda? Dr. Malek said that he was thirsty and that he would indeed enjoy a nice soda. Then without getting up and by raising his voice just a little, the official turned toward the kitchen and said, "Bring Dr. Malek a soda." A minute later, a tray came floating into the living room with a bottle of Coke on it. Dr. Malek looked at the man, who smiled gently and nodded for him to take it, and then reached up and took the bottle off the tray. The tray floated slowly back into the kitchen.

I'm not asking you to believe this; I am asking you to understand that millions of people in the world have a worldview that can explain it and that when it comes to demons versus Jesus, Jesus wins. Dr. Malek told that story to teach his American audience that there are a lot more spiritual activities going on in the world than what we were used to seeing and that the Holy Spirit power available to Christians is the most effective way to combat them. The question I never thought to ask him is, why would you want to combat them if they bring you Cokes?

That brings us to the darker side of the power encounter and why it's spiritual warfare. Most of the stories aren't as friendly as Dawn's and Dr. Malek's. A Pentecostal pastor friend of mine who lived in New Haven, Connecticut, told of his experiences in a house owned by a woman in her fifties. There was tapping on the walls all night and other "activity"; scared, the owner had locked herself in just two rooms of this huge old three-story home. The house was full of vintage clothing, bottles of Scotch from the early 1900s, and World War II weapons. An artistic community wanted to turn the old home into a dance studio and, not knowing about any of the spiritual activity, offered to buy it. The woman agreed to sell it on the spot and was gone, leaving all the contents. The new owners went through all the old stuff and sold some, but they kept the Scotch, and the dancers kept most of the clothing. After they moved in, they noticed footsteps in the hallways, knocking on all four walls of a room when nobody was close by, and objects being moved around from one place to another. They invited a Pentecostal Christian friend who had been involved with the occult (specifically, in a coven of witches and as a practitioner of paranormal "magick") to come over, and as soon as she walked in, she said, "There are a lot of beings here. There's a lot going on. It will take a long time to get them to go and to clean this house up." As of this writing, they are still doing spiritual warfare, although the paranormal activity in the house is gradually lessening.

Another Pentecostal friend of mine, Nadira, struggled with ridiculously violent and horrible dreams while living in a rented house. She dreamed of battles and warfare and of her husband being imprisoned for things he didn't do, such as raping another woman. She was terrified to go to sleep, yet she had to. She would often wake up from these nightmares and have her husband pray for her, but she could not go back to sleep and would lie awake all night. This happened every night for a couple of months, and it was completely impairing her life. A friend suggested that they have a "warfare night" to battle the spiritual oppression that was in their home. So a few days later, about twenty young Pentecostals came over to hang out for the evening. They started by having dinner together, and then some of the break dancers pushed back the furniture in the living room and taught some of the others how to break dance. Several of the people were missionaries, and some of the others did ministry through music and drama. After eating and then dancing together for a while, Nadira and her husband told them all what had been happening and expressed their thanks that everyone had come over to pray for them.

The group fanned out throughout the house and yard, finding every nook and cranny, and prayed for the Spirit of the living God to be present in this home and in this family. Some walked the perimeter of the land, others shimmied into the crawl space under the house, and some went into the basement, which could be accessed only from the outside through a very small door. They went into every room and anointed every door frame in the house with olive oil. It was a free-for-all; the participants did their own thing, and there was no direction or planning—just twenty people praying their own prayers in their own ways for a more peaceful and healthy home. One sat in a corner the whole time; another lay on the floor crying. They told the devil to leave, that he had no authority in this house because Nadira and her family were believers in Jesus, and that the nightmares had to end.

After an hour of intense prayer and physically touching almost every inch of the property, they gathered back together in the living room to reflect and share. One person said he felt like there had been abuse of Native Americans on the land, that blood had been spilled, and that maybe there were spirits who had been wounded, hurt, or oppressed. Others talked about binding the spirit of fear and casting it out. Then to lighten the mood, one said, "And then the angel in the ball of fire in the backyard shot fire at our butts." After that, they had a "worship night," singing worship songs and entering into jubilant upbeat "worship warfare." Think hip-hop in praise of God. The night ended in celebration and thankfulness for what God had done. After that, Nadira says, "I never had nightmares again." It worked.[2]

Some Pentecostals believe that there are territorial spirits—demons that control certain areas of geographical land, like southern Sudan or upstate New York. For instance, a missionary to the Philippines tells of his ministry and travels around Pennsylvania:

I remember ministering in a region of Pennsylvania once a week for about six months. The area must have covered about 400–500 square miles. Each week I was usually in a different town. After I entered the home of the person who was to receive ministry, I would discover each person beginning to suffer from the same symptoms. They were experiencing fear, an upset stomach and buzzing in their ears. The buzzing made them feel dizzy and confused. After three cases in a row, I directed my attention to the spirit causing this phenomenon and found that I was dealing with a territorial spirit that ruled over the whole area. He did not like what I was doing. My ministry was a threat to his rule over the people of that region. He cursed me in their minds and sometimes spoke out of their mouths. Knowing what I was dealing with, I broke this spirit's power over each individual and commanded him to leave. Immediately, their physical and emotional symptoms disappeared and I was able to continue to minister and witness them set free from the powers of darkness oppressing them.

Generations of witchcraft were practiced throughout the area. It was practiced in the form of psychic healing that had religious packaging. This ruling spirit was very powerful and made claims upon a number of generations. One day, as I was ministering to a former Satanist, the territorial ruler manifested himself in the countenance of the individual. The face contorted and a raspy, sneering voice shouted out, "I have been resisting you as you ministered to Mary _____, Edward _____, Jason _____ and Sheila _____ and many others. You have invaded my territory and I will fight you so they will not be set free of my power over them. If you do not stop, I will attack your wife and your children and I will destroy you. Your God will not be able to protect you from my powers!"

It was surprising to hear a powerful spirit speak out and begin naming people to whom I was ministering. The person he was speaking through did not even know any of them. The enemy tries to intimidate with threats in an attempt to force God's servants to back off. In reality, the spirits are afraid they are going to lose their power base and their ability to rule over people. They recognize and fear the authority of Christ that you represent. Long ago, I learned to trust the Lord for both myself and my family. He has never failed me.[3]

Other Pentecostals don't take the territorial aspect as seriously, but they still believe that demonic activity is real and that Christians are called to spiritual warfare.[4] Spiritual warfare is defined by the Assemblies of God as countering "attacks of Satan" through prayer, fasting, and casting out demons. They teach that the gift of discernment of spirits is available for those instances when a greater understanding of the immediate presence and power of Satan is essential. We have concerns about those who regularly teach and practice an arrogant, presumptuous involvement with satanic powers. Certainly, we need to be cautious of the evil one's traps. For the Bible says he is deceptive and comes as a 'roaring lion' eager to devour. Yet we are to have no fear of Satan or of his efforts to seduce and destroy God's children. Scripture teaches us that if we resist the devil he will flee from us (James 4:7). . . . Satan is real, but experiencing the presence and power of an omnipotent yet personal God is the privilege of all Spirit-filled believers."[5]

In cultures around the world where spirituality has been a deep part of life for thousands of years, it makes sense to rely on God's power available in Jesus to counter the evil powers that seek to "steal, kill, and destroy."[6]

Pentecostals in Haiti relate to the practitioners of voodoo by "beating them at their own game"; the Pentecostals return the curses they receive with powerful blessings and counterprayers intended to neutralize and overpower the spells. Pentecostals live in a very similar world, the biblical world, and have explanations for these things—they're demons. But they're not afraid, because demons don't have the last word; Jesus conquered death, hell, and the grave in his life, death, and resurrection, so there's nothing to fear. "For God has not given us the spirit of fear, but of power and love and a sound mind."[7]

Most Pentecostals teach that the "most important thing in spiritual warfare is the power found in the name of Jesus Christ. . . . It is the strongest weapon in spiritual warfare."[8] David Yonggi Cho is the pastor of the largest church in the world, a Pentecostal church in South Korea with about eight hundred thousand members. He prays for people to be healed by warring in the spiritual realm and saying, "You, filthy Satan, I command you in the *name of Jesus of Nazareth*, be driven out from the saint."[9] Nak-hyung

Kim, a dentist who is an elder in Cho's church, "says that he can see when the power of bad spirits is harassing a patient during an operation. Then, he commands, 'Filthy demons, come out in the name of the Lord, Jesus.' In many cases, the [fully conscious] patient regains faith, and the operation is finished success-fully."[10] We might be a little disturbed if our dentist started talk-ing to demons while we were having a root canal, but I know Pentecostal Christians who seek out Christian doctors who are willing to pray with their patients before, during, and after the surgeries they perform. That holistic approach to medicine is related to a holistic approach to power and warfare—they're as spiritual as they are physical.

Power and Spirits in the Bible

Jesus was both a peacemaker and a divine warrior against the powers of evil. He crushed evil not with violence but with exorcisms, deliverance, healings, and forgiveness. Pentecostals around the world, but especially in the global South, pick up on the power of Jesus' ministry against demonic power and accept it as a powerful way to deliver people today from addictions and disease, especially since the disciples in Acts followed in Jesus' footsteps and had spiritual power encounters themselves. There are dozens of exorcism stories in scripture, and it's been widely noted that the Bible is so influential in Africa and Asia because "it describes a world which is immediately recognizable."[11]

The African and Asian worldview is a reality that is very similar to the Bible, and that reality is quite foreign to some Americans and Europeans. For instance, a white middle-class pastor from the United States visited South Africa and wan-dered into a black church there. When the people found out he was an ordained pastor from America, they told their pastor, and their pastor announced to the congregation, "Oh, my friends, I have wonderful news for you. Pastor Smith has come to visit us all the way from the United States. I'm going to invite him to conduct tonight's exorcism."[12] Pastor Smith had never cast out any demons before, but he did just fine.

Exorcism is a regular part of African, Asian, South American, and biblical Christianity. What does the Bible say about power, demons, and spiritual warfare?

Mark has this to say: One day Jesus was teaching in a synagogue and transforming the people with his wisdom and authority; not only was he a good speaker, but what he said also had a depth that compelled people to reflection and action. Suddenly, "a man in their synagogue who was possessed by an evil spirit cried out, 'What do you want with us, Jesus of Nazareth? Have you come to destroy us? I know who you are— the Holy One of God!'"[13]

Let's stop here for a minute. We in the West know that such things don't really happen, or if they do, the man probably suffered from a psychological or emotional disorder that we could diagnose and treat. It's also possible that Mark and Luke and Matthew just made up these stories to strengthen their case for Jesus. There is much critical discourse regarding these stories, and Western scholars have been demythologizing them for centuries, getting rid of the mythical aspects to find the real meaning. Like most well-educated Westerners, I was taught in a non-Pentecostal graduate school not to take any of these stories at face value. Yet I express these doubts a little bit tongue-in-cheek, because the arrogant dismissals of the spiritual reality are often kindly and patiently tolerated by people who have seen trays float through the air with freshly opened Coke bottles on them.

We can dismiss the stories of deliverance in the Bible and the stories of deliverance in the twenty-first century, but acceptance of them is one reason Pentecostalism is one of the world's fastest-growing faiths—it fits extremely well with some cultures' sense of reality. As noted by Allan Anderson, a leading scholar of global Pentecostalism, "A major reason for the attraction of Pentecostal churches for people oriented to popular religiosity is a sympathetic or at least a serious approach by Pentecostal preachers to African life and culture, fears and uncertainties, and the worldview of spirits, magic and witchcraft."[14]

Now back to our story. Jesus turned to the man and addressed the spirit sternly and directly: "Be quiet! Come out of him!" The evil spirit shook the man violently and came out of him with an ear-piercing shriek. The people witnessing this were so amazed and stunned at Jesus' spiritual strength that they debated with one another, "What is this? A new teaching with authority! He even gives orders to unclean spirits and they obey him!"[15] The word spread rapidly around Galilee that this carpenter from Nazareth was saying and doing some pretty amazing things—healing diseases and driving out "many demons." Jesus was bringing the good news of the kingdom of God to suffering people, liberating and delivering them.

Another time Jesus traveled to a burial ground, a cemetery full of tombs where demon-possessed people lived isolated and alone. One of the men there was famous because "no one could bind him anymore, not even with a chain. For he had often been chained hand and foot, but he tore the chains apart and broke the irons on his feet. No one was strong enough to subdue him. Night and day among the tombs and in the hills he would cry out and cut himself with stones."[16] Jesus sought out this most distraught and tortured man and said, "Come out of him, you evil spirit!" But the spirits responded with a request that Jesus not torture them, so Jesus asked them their name and found out that this was Legion, "for we are many." They begged Jesus repeatedly not to drive them out of the area and asked instead to be sent into a herd of pigs (remember that from a Jewish perspective, pigs were unclean, inedible, useless animals). Jesus allowed them to go into the herd of two thousand pigs that then promptly rushed headlong down a steep hillside into the sea and drowned. The pig herders rushed into the "town and countryside" to tell everybody what happened to the famous demon-possessed man and to their expensive herd of pigs. "When they came to Jesus, they saw the very man who had been possessed by a legion of demons, sitting there, dressed and in his right mind; and they were afraid."[17] They begged Jesus to leave their area, and the now healthy and demon-free man asked to go with him, but Jesus said, "Go home to your family and tell them how much the Lord has done for you, and how he has had mercy on you." So the man did exactly what Jesus told him to do—he went throughout the ten cities of the surrounding area amazing people with his testimony of deliverance that came at the merciful command of Jesus of Nazareth.

Jesus obviously had his enemies, both Gentile pig herders and Jewish lawyers. Attorneys and professors in Jerusalem accused him of being able to drive out lesser and weaker demons because he was possessed with the powerful prince of demons—Beelzebub. They could not argue with the evidence that people were miraculously freed from wandering around naked in the graveyards and were in their right minds and reconciled with their families. So they instead challenged his credibility and said he himself was possessed with "an evil spirit." But Jesus said that accusing him of working for the devil was as close to blasphemy as one could get. On the contrary, Jesus' exorcisms consistently led to reunited families and greater health and well-being (except perhaps for the pigs).

Pentecostal history is full of stories of other Christians and religious people accusing Pentecostals of being demon-possessed and working for the devil. Many books have even been written about it, from A. M. Hills's *Pentecost Rejected* (1902) to John MacArthur's *Charismatic Chaos* (1993). But Pentecostals believe they are doing what Jesus did and what he taught his disciples to do. At the end of his gospel account, Mark tells us that Jesus said to his followers, "And these signs will accompany those who believe: In my name they will drive out demons; they will speak in new tongues; and they will pick up snakes with their hands; and when they drink deadly poison, it will not hurt them at all; they will place their hands on sick people, and they will get well."[18] This is the Pentecostal mandate for powerful living and spiritual warfare—it comes straight from the mouth of Jesus and is written in the "red letters" of the New Testament. Most Pentecostal scholars acknowledge that this saying was not original to Mark and was added later, but some contend that that might just mean that Jesus did say it, but Mark forgot to write it down, and when it matched their exorcism, faith-healing, tongue-talking experiences, the early church added it.

Those experiences are recorded in the Acts of the Apostles, the story of the explosive growth of the early church that functions as the blueprint and inspiration for Pentecostal living. Each time the church advanced into a new geographical region, "Acts shows confrontation with the evil spirit-powers as the first stage of ministry in the evangelistic spread of the gospel."[19] Jesus had said, "You will receive power and you will become my witnesses," and that is exactly the story that Acts tells.

Acts tells the story of a sorcerer named Simon who amazed people with his magic and the disciples healing people and casting out demons. Philip had come to town and was teaching about Jesus and performing miraculous signs: "with shrieks, evil spirits came out of many, and many paralytics and cripples were healed. So there was great joy in that city." Simon, who presented himself in the area as "the divine power known as the Great Power," asked to buy the more powerful power that the Jesus people had so that he too could lay his hands on people so they could "receive the Holy Spirit." Peter rebuked him and told him that he couldn't buy the gift of God with money but that he should repent and ask for forgiveness. This power encounter between a well-known sorcerer and the followers of Jesus is the model that Pentecostal Christians follow. Preach the good news of Jesus, lay hands on people for their healings and deliverance, and when you're opposed by other power brokers with vested interests in controlling the community, reveal that your power is greater and invite them to repent and follow Jesus. And there's no need to be scared, for Jesus said, "Fear not. . . . I am with you always."[20]

It's not all rosy, though. Later in Acts, Paul is confronted by a sorcerer named Elymas, who is trying to prevent the proconsul (a governor) from converting to Christianity. "Paul, filled with the Holy Spirit, looked straight at Elymas and said, 'You are a child of the devil and an enemy of everything that is right! You are full of all kinds of deceit and trickery. Now the hand of the Lord is against you. You are going to be blind, and for a time you will be unable to see the light of the sun."[21] Elymas ended up blind and became a believer, "for he was amazed at the teaching about the Lord."

Some time later, Paul's success at driving out demons in the name of Jesus was copied by some people who were not Christians. Seven sons of a local priest in Ephesus would say, "In the name of Jesus, whom Paul preaches, I command you to come out." But one day the evil spirit answered them by saying, "Jesus I know, and Paul I know, but who are you?" Then the demon-possessed man attacked them and "gave them such a beating that they ran out of the house naked and bleeding." Almost needless to say, "The word of the Lord spread widely and grew in power."[22]

These stories are so familiar to Pentecostals from sermons and Bible studies that they can use them as campaign slogans. My hall mates in college helped me run for student congress by coming up with posters that referenced both me and the other candidate: "Jesus I know, and Paul I know, but who's Larry?" It was funny to us, but we decided not to use them outside of just our dorm because it was a little too disrespectful. Nevertheless, most Pentecostals would get the joke because Pentecostals preach and live the exorcism and power encounter stories in the Bible.

What Are the Problems?

There are two main areas where Pentecostals need to be careful regarding power and spiritual warfare. First, when life is viewed as a power encounter and triumph is always assured because of Jesus Christ, it is difficult for Pentecostals to handle failure, defeat, and suffering. Yet Jesus failed, was defeated, and suffered. Jesus ultimately overcame death through the resurrection, but he failed to change the world completely, was defeated (at least temporarily) through torture and murder, and suffered terribly along the way. Life wasn't tremendously better for many of his followers; the Bible is a narrative of setbacks, suffering, and incomplete victories as well as powerful successes. Critics have noted that Pentecostals tend to be "triumphalistic" and expect Holy Spirit power always to win. This can be a real problem; it sets them up for a potential fall when the triumph is not forthcoming. All triumph and no loss does not square with the Bible or our reality, so Pentecostals need to be careful to recognize that sometimes God is with us in our sufferings and does not always deliver us from them.

The second problem is that Pentecostals can develop "demon vision" and begin seeing demons everywhere. Frank Peretti's best-seller *This Present Darkness* told the story of a small American town where Christians battled a New Age takeover attempt of their college by praying in support of the angels who were combating the demons. The muscled, sword-carrying, winged, flying angels had names like Tal (a Native American angel) and Guilo, while the sulfur-breathing demons crouched in corners, possessed people, and could sink their claws into your skull to cause you to have a headache. Here's how Peretti described these demonic creatures:

> Could anyone have seen him, the initial impression would not have been so much his reptilian, warted appearance as the way his figure seemed to absorb light and not return it, as if he were more a shadow than an object, a strange, animated hole in space. But this little spirit was invisible to the eyes of men, unseen and immaterial, drifting over the town, banking one way and then the other, guided by will and not wind, his swirling wings quivering in a grayish blur as they propelled him. He was like a high-strung little gargoyle, his hide a slimy, bottomless black, his body thin and spiderlike: half humanoid, half animal, totally demon. Two huge yellow cat-eyes bulged out of his face, darting

to and fro, peering, searching. His breath came in short, sulfurous gasps, visible as glowing yellow vapor. He was carefully watching and following his charge, the driver of a brown Buick moving through the streets of Ashton far below.[23]

I read this book when I was fifteen years old and loved it— but it also scared me. I remember reading late at night in my room with all the lights on and stopping to pray in tongues and in the name of Jesus to get all the demons out of my room (even the little ones). When I went to a Pentecostal college a few years later, *This Present Darkness* was required reading in freshman English. Having already read it, I recognized how well it matched my theology and understanding of the world. Peretti's novel simply told a story, maybe with a little exaggeration, that reflected what many Pentecostals, at least to some degree, already believed. Pentecostals "have built an intriguing and elaborate system of demonology"[24] and this particular manifestation of it sold several million copies and stayed on the Christian Bookseller's Association's top-ten best-sellers list for 150 consecutive weeks. I no longer share Peretti's demonology, for I now have more of an integrated Christian worldview—I see the spiritual and physical as two aspects of the same reality.[25]

But seeing demons is problematic only for people who think they're really not there. In other words, if they are really there, then the ones who know how to deal with them powerfully are the ones in tune with reality. As Mark Twain said, "It ain't what you don't know that gets you into trouble. It's what you know for sure that just ain't so." This is the Pentecostal explanation for why their experiences and their reading of the Bible work so well: Pentecostals know things about the spirit world that other people have convinced themselves "just ain't so." Combine this with another Mark Twain observation, and the appeal of Pentecostalism packs an even greater punch: "It ain't those parts of the Bible that I can't understand that bother me; it's the parts that I do understand." The biblical stories and teachings about power over the devil are pretty straightforward in many people's minds, and that bothers a lot of Christians, because they don't want to think about what it would be like to live in a world that is really inhabited by demons and ghosts. But Pentecostals just accept it and run with it.

What's the Appeal?

Pentecostalism is growing around the world because Pentecostals take power and spiritual warfare seriously and can battle powerfully in the spiritual realm, with physically visible results. People who already believe in the reality of demons and angels are well prepared for Pentecostalism, not because Pentecostalism is the only religion that accepts their reality but because Pentecostalism has the reality of the demonic more central in their worldview. As one sociologist says, it's a "tough Christianity" that believes in deliverance from the evil spirits that bring sickness, poverty, disease, pollution, violence, and substance abuse.[26]

What exactly do we mean when we say Pentecostalism is "tough" Christianity? We mean strong and powerful enough to be able to take on demonic manifestations and curses that lock your jaw shut. A Pentecostal pastor in Tanzania is very careful about who else he lets minister in his local area. My cousin in Tanzania told me about a newbie who came to preach in this pastor's region. The new preacher hadn't prepared himself spiritually with prayer and fasting. As he was lying in bed his first night, his jaw moved to the side and locked up completely, and he could not talk. The local pastor prayed for him and reversed the curse but told him that next time he comes, he had better be ready. This same pastor also battled a thirty-foot-high smoky demon that a shaman conjured up. After the pastor destroyed it by praying in the name of Jesus, the entire village and the shaman himself converted to Pentecostalism.[27] This is so clearly visible in Africa because Pentecostalism fits with the

"African map of the universe."[28] Ogbu Kalu, an African scholar of Pentecostalism, describes the African worldview:

> Reality is divided into two: the human world and the spirit world. . . . The three dimensions of space are the sky, the earth (consisting of land and water), and the ancestral or spirit world. . . . There are human spirits on land because each human being has a guardian spirit. . . . [There are] ancestral spirits and spiritual forces, which individuals can acquire through rituals for enhancing life force. Witchcraft is the use of human psychic power to do evil. . . . Evil forces are without bodily forms, so they can embody people, animals, and physical objects, and manipulate these to harm people.[29]

Modernity has taught us not to believe in spirits, angels, and demons, and many Christian missions denied their existence in their attempts to evangelize Africa, Asia, and Latin America, and this denial left them relatively weak. But "the Pentecostal goes through life keenly aware of the presence of evil forces just as the African does."[30]

Pentecostalism is appealing to so many because it acknowledges the reality of the spirit world and the occult in daily life and adopts a spiritual warfare approach that "reclaims God's rule over the whole inhabited earth."[31] This is important because it recognizes that God is bigger than the problems that work against people. The Genesis story of Moses and the snakes in Egypt helps us see the unique appeal of Pentecostalism. Pharaoh's sorcerers turned their sticks into snakes to show the power of Egypt and to intimidate Moses. But Moses turned his stick into a snake that then ate their snakes.

The approach to spiritual worldviews that says, "We know this isn't real. People aren't really demon-possessed or affected by curses," would have responded, "That's not magic; that's just sleight of hand. You didn't really turn your sticks into snakes.

I'm smarter than that." Churches and religions with that approach are not very appealing to people who regularly see and experience the reality of demon possession. Pentecostalism is more like Moses' response: "So what that you turned your sticks into snakes? Now watch mine eat yours!" It's a power encounter that recognizes the power of the other but shows that our God is more powerful. The attractive and transformative message is that no curse from anybody, whether inherited from your parents or brought about through your own sins, has ultimate power over your life. You can be delivered by the power of the Spirit from any attacks against you. As one popular African hymn goes, "Jesus has come and Satan has run away!" Pentecostals know the power of names and learn to "speak the reversal to curses by using the name of Jesus, and the blood and the resources of the Holy Spirit."[32] This powerful message that embraces and accepts power encounters in a victorious way is a message of hope and joy.

But Africa is one thing; what about America? Did you ever see the television show *Touched by an Angel?* Odds are that you have seen it, since almost 60 percent of Americans watched that show during its run.[33] But do you really believe in angels and demons, spirits of some kind floating or walking around that we can't see (at least most of the time)? Odds are that you do, since according to a recent poll, the *majority* of Christians and non-Christians alike believe that "angels and demons are active in the world today."[34] Furthermore, the popularity of paranormal shows like *Ghost Hunters, Medium,* and *Psychic Investigators* (psychics helping solve criminal cases) buttresses the studies showing that many Americans believe in the paranormal. The most comprehensive survey of paranormal beliefs and experiences ever, administered to a random national sample, showed that an astounding 45 percent of folks who live on the East Coast of the United States believe that places can be haunted.[35] Non-Christians rank the highest on the "paranormal beliefs scale," and Evangelical Protestants rank the lowest.[36] Pentecostals are most like those who chose "other religions" or "no religion" on the survey when it comes to belief in the supernatural; this means that Pentecostals are dissimilar to American Evangelicals and more similar to the nonreligious folks they would like to convert.

I recently heard from a friend that her eight-year-old son was having trouble going to sleep at night because he was afraid he would have nightmares. Every night she prayed with him, talked rationally with him, read to him, snuggled with him, and talked and prayed with him some more. But nothing was working. Night after night he kept resisting sleep because of fear, sometimes staying up as late as 1:30 A.M. Eventually one night his grand-mother, a longtime Pentecostal, prayed out loud in an authoritative voice, "Satan we command you in the name of Jesus to get out of this room and quit bothering this boy! You have no right to be here; you have been defeated by Jesus. Go back to hell where you came from right now, in the name of *Jesus!*" I admit that this is a little bit creepy, if not bizarre. The boy had not been raised to think that there would be demons in his room, but that forceful and direct order from his grandmother calmed him, and he relaxed and went to sleep (of course, now he has to deal with what in the world it means to have the devil in his room).

What's the appeal? People whose lives have been changed are all around, just like the demon-possessed man in the tombs who went home to his family and the whole village saw it and heard about it. When those who live under bondage are set free, they are encouraged to tell others about it, just like Jesus encouraged the liberated man to "tell how much the Lord has done for you." While we might think that Pentecostalism is a private matter between individuals and their God, these deliverances are public events with far-ranging effects. When Philip went to Samaria, "evil spirits came out of many" and "there was great joy in the city." The Pentecostal movement spread through many countries in Africa as Charismatic young people resisted the non-Christian communal "witchcraft-cleansing" rituals in their villages. One group of youths near Umuahia, Nigeria, was reprimanded severely by parents, elders, priests, and even church members for not participating, but they held fast. On the day of the ceremony, with the entire village gathered for the oath, the young people instead went into a church "to pray against the deity and neutralize its hold on the community."[37] The elders erupted into a violent quarrel, the ceremony was disrupted and ruined, the "compromising ethics of the members of the mainline churches" were exposed, and the youths led the village into Pentecostal revival.

Skeptics can doubt, but Pentecostalism encounters the powers on their own turf and fits better than any other kind of Christianity into widespread worldviews that accept the reality of the supernatural. By answering the questions many cultures have about spirits and oppression, it opens up the possibility for a life of power and liberation for those who believe.

CHAPTER 7

PROPHECY, VISIONS, AND DREAMS

Your sons and your daughters will prophesy!
Your young people will see visions and
your old people will dream dreams!
—*Peter's sermon, Acts 2*

I once taught at a Pentecostal college in Texas, where my theological and political leanings were sometimes problematic for its leaders. In 2003, I signed a letter (written by Pentecostal ministers) asking President Bush not to invade Iraq.[1] I also annually (and unsuccessfully) encouraged our school's administration to observe Martin Luther King Jr. Day. In response, I was reprimanded for opposing the Iraq war, and the board of regents unanimously passed a resolution to "express concern regarding any faculty member taking a public stand in opposition to the war situation currently facing America." In 2004, Carissa, a friend of my wife's and mine, had a dream about visiting the college where I taught (also her alma mater) and trying to find my office. In her dream, she walked through the classrooms but couldn't find me. She did, however, see one of the faculty members most opposed to my concern regarding the Iraq war. He was having a party in his classroom, and there were cupcakes. She eventually found my class, but I wasn't there. My students said to her, "Haven't you heard? You need to go talk to him." When she found me, I was taking boxes out of my office, and I said that the college had asked me to leave. I said that my family was OK but that some things had happened, and I was not going to say anything bad about them. In her dream, she knew that her uncle was significantly involved somehow, and we sat outside my office and talked about the situation. I was getting ready to go home and tell Deborah, my wife. In the dream, it just seemed like the right time to leave; it "really stunk" and was very hurtful, but there was an underlying sense of peace.

The next day, Carissa called to tell me about her dream and said that she felt I needed to leave the school. Her uncle was still pastoring a church in Washington, so his role in the dream didn't make a lot of sense to us at the time. She didn't tell anyone else about the dream.

I knew she was right about finding another job, so a year later, I applied for a position at a university in California with the hopes of having a bit more academic freedom. While I was waiting to hear, Carissa's uncle, who had become my dean, asked me to come to his office for a chat. He and I go way back; he was one of my favorite professors when I was a student, and we worked together when I was in student congress and he was vice president for student services. I had been very pleased that he had come back to be our new dean. When I walked into his office, he smiled at me and held up his two fists as far apart as he could reach and said, "Paul, the president is over here and you are over there. And it doesn't seem like either one of you is going to change." He went on to tell me that I would not be getting another faculty contract for the following year and that I needed to find another job.

I was so preoccupied with this startling news that I pretty much kept it to myself. A few days later, Carissa, who had no idea about what was going on and the stress we were under, called to tell me about another dream she had had on Good Friday. She had dreamed that we were all in a big room together, catching up and having a great time. Deborah was glowing with happiness, and we were amazed at how great life was. In the dream, Carissa talked mostly to Deborah, and there was a strong feeling that we were where we were supposed to be, fulfilling our dreams. After quietly listening to her recounting her dream, I told her that her uncle had informed me I wouldn't be getting another faculty contract and that I had an interview with a university in California three days later.

Those are, as far as I know, the only two dreams Carissa has ever had about Deborah and me, and we've known her since 1998. The first one was oddly accurate, two years in advance, and the second one was incredibly timely. I did indeed get the wonderful job in California. And people there observe Martin Luther King Jr. Day!

I do not offer this story as evidence to prove that God speaks through dreams; I know better than to try to prove that. Rather, I offer it as a true testimony of Pentecostal openness to and experience of prophecy, dreams, and visions. This openness is one of the most appealing aspects of Pentecostalism and allies it with the beliefs of the majority of people in the world. The majority of Americans, from 52 percent in the West to 61 percent in the East, believe that "dreams can sometimes foretell the future or reveal hidden truths."[2] Forty-three percent of all Americans claim to have actually had a dream that later came true—that's 129 million people.[3] Pentecostals are even more convinced that divine revelations occur through prophecy, dreams, and visions. The statistics show that throughout the world, they are two to five times more likely than the average Christian to report that they have "received a direct revelation from God."[4] It's not the dreams per se that are distinctive to Pentecostals; it's their belief that God can and will still speak to them individually.

Mia Sherwood is a Pentecostal with a prophetic dream ministry—she interprets people's dreams and helps them understand what God may be saying to them. At her dream interpretation

Web site, she shares her simple motto, "Hearing from God through our dreams and visions." She explains the process like this:

> Our mission is to teach people to hear from God for themselves. We are all capable of hearing directly from God, and a very under-rated way is through our dreams. Our mission is to encourage you with our examples and to use our examples to help you hear from God through interpreting your dreams. . . . We don't pretend to know what every dream means, but sometimes the Holy Spirit does give us the interpretation. If He does, we will be happy to send you the interpretation via e-mail. Otherwise, we will plainly tell you that we don't have the interpretation but we will be happy to answer questions and discuss what the symbols probably mean. Click here to submit your dream.[5]

Most Pentecostals have dreams with prophetic meaning. My wife, Deborah, sometimes dreams that her Grandpa Bird dies—he was a Pentecostal minister for over fifty years and still lives in a small town in East Texas. But each time she has that dream, we find out within a few days that somebody we know or a friend of the family has died. She didn't really notice until the second time it happened. Then we talked about it and thought what an odd coincidence it was. A couple of years later, she had another dream in which Grandpa Bird died, and she told me the next morning. We realized that now we'd see if it was coincidence or not. Sure enough, the next day her mom called and said that a close friend of the family had passed away. In the course of our sixteen years of marriage, this has happened five times.

Prophecy, Visions, and Divine Revelation

Prophecy is closely related to dreams and visions, because they are all forms of the Pentecostal belief that God is speaking to human beings directly, not just through scripture. One lay Pentecostal who tries to help others understand prophecy describes it simply as "when the Holy Spirit puts an idea in your mind and you share it with one or more people. God puts the idea in your mind and you put it in your own words."[6] That is also how many Christians think the Bible was written: God gave the writers ideas, and they wrote in their own words. So whether it comes as a direct thought from God in your own head, through an event or another person, or in a direct vision or dream, God is speaking.

Prophets speak to people on behalf of God, but they have to pray and listen carefully to hear from God first before they can speak. One Pentecostal preacher compares it to a satellite and a receiver dish: many people may have a dish, but it has to be turned on and pointed in the right direction to receive the signal;[7] only then can it broadcast the message it has received to other people who are listening or watching. Yet contrary to popular understanding, Pentecostals do not commonly expect prophecy to predict the future. Prophecy is instead usually a message that provides insight, assurance, confirmation, warning, or direction.[8]

Don, a Pentecostal Christian, told me that a woman in his church has always been sort of his "personal prophet." At significant points in his life, Regina seemed to have an uncanny ability to provide a timely "prophetic nugget" for him. On one particularly striking occasion, when he was serving as youth pastor, he was struggling privately with whether or not to take a position at the denominational headquarters. He felt torn between the strong feelings that God had called him as a pastor and this other opportunity that seemed to be presenting itself. Was it God leading? Or was it temptation to leave his ministry and calling? He wasn't sure. He kept this all to himself.

Then one day he got a call from Regina. "Hey, Don, I had a dream about you the other night and think I should share it with you. It started with me walking into my house, and there you are, lying asleep on my couch. My first thought was, 'This is uncharacteristic of Don; he doesn't sleep; he's a hard worker;

he's diligent. Something odd is going on here.' A kid in the youth group was also there, and he says, 'Let's wake him up.' So we start shaking you, but you don't budge. Then the teenager says, 'He's not asleep; he's on drugs.' Now Don, at that point the dream stops, and I wake up. I have this sense that God is telling you something but that your work with the young people is like a drug and you're drugged up and not listening."

Don told her he appreciated her call and then put it aside, as Pentecostals are taught to do. We are told to weigh any "word of wisdom" or "word of knowledge" or prophecy along with other factors and other input. The book of Proverbs says there is wisdom in a multitude of counselors. So he shelved the idea, since he had not even applied for the job yet; he was still praying and thinking about it. But a few weeks later, headquarters called him and offered him the position. He told me, "At that point, I combined my personal experiences and feelings with Regina's prophecy. But her prophetic dream, that prophetic voice, weighed heavily in my decision to take that job. God was telling me something that I clearly wasn't able to hear—'it's OK if you don't continue the work here; I appreciate what you've done, but it's OK to move on.'" Then, in answer to the topic of this entire book, he added, "Why am I a Pentecostal? Because stuff like that happens."[9]

It's not uncommon for Pentecostals of all sorts to have prophetic leadings. One day I was sitting in my office at the university, and Blake, one of my students, walked in. He had been in a couple of my classes, we had talked about his spiritual life and other issues many times at his request, and we had a good relationship. He had arrived at the Christian university as a hard-drinking, womanizing, all-night-partying athlete. But during his first semester, he experienced a dramatic conversion and call to full-time Christian ministry that rocked his world. He gave up his old habits, surrounded himself with new friends, became an amazingly different person, and a couple of years later married Sarah. Together they were about to graduate and go into the ministry. But when he came into my office that day, something didn't seem quite right.

We made small talk about how I was doing and how he was doing. But when he would make eye contact with me, I felt as though I should really be his friend and say something I had never said to anyone before in my life. He had invited my input into his life, and I had been discipling him through readings, prayer, and conversation, but this was a completely different feeling for me. So I looked him in the eye and gently said, "Blake, are you struggling with pornography?" He said no but continued to hold my gaze. I then realized what he was struggling with and said, "Are you cheating on your wife?" He said yes.

We sat in silence for a moment and just looked at each other. Then I asked him if he had told her, if Sarah knew. He said he had not and she did not and asked what I thought he should do. I told him he knew what I thought and he knew what he should do, and this led into a three-hour conversation there in my office as all the details and rationalizations flooded out. Eventually he decided that he was willing to tell Sarah if I would go with him and be there for both of them. I told him I definitely would. Within a couple of minutes, there was a knock on my door. Through the window in the door we saw Sarah, looking determined, fearful, and suspicious. Blake said, "I guess this is how we do it." So I got up and welcomed Sarah, closed the door, and spent the rest of the evening (and the next several months) with them as they worked to restore their relationship—unfortunately to no avail; they ultimately divorced.

My feeling of certainty that led me to question Blake about adultery is not a common occurrence in my life. But among Pentecostals, we would call that the "gift of discernment" or prophetic insight. It doesn't mean that I am a special prophet; Pentecostals believe that anyone, anywhere, of any age, gender, experience, or educational level can be used by God to speak the right prophetic word at the right time. That is democracy of the Holy Spirit—everybody has a voice. This democratizing move of God in Pentecost, where sons, daughters, slaves, free, young, and old can all prophesy, dream, and have visions, is empowering women and other traditionally excluded groups around the globe. It is a clear indicator of why the movement is so appealing and growing so fast. The more people you believe can lead, the more potential leaders you can have. The more people your movement believes can participate and be empowered to speak for God, the more people will do so. By not limiting the voice of God to males or the seminary-educated, Pentecostalism radically expands the possibilities of who can and will hear from God and speak to the rest of us when we need it.

Prophecy in Pentecostalism is not just one on one; it can also attract huge throngs and work on a large scale. Both self-proclaimed and organizationally licensed prophets travel from church to church offering prophetic ministry or draw crowds at their own churches. There *are* charlatans who fleece the sheep with false and generic prophecies. But there are also authentic Christians who speak words of wisdom and insight into people's lives, live quite simply and humbly, and still maintain ministries that reach thousands of people at a time.

One such story of divine revelation is the life of Margaret Wanjiru. Margaret grew up in the slums of Nairobi, Kenya, in a polygamous family with an alcoholic father. She was pregnant at sixteen and again at seventeen and became involved in witchcraft, along with her sisters and mother. Her mom took care of her two children, and she finished school and got a job as a model, but she was fired after an altercation with her boss. After several more rough years of changing employment, failed business ventures, and deep involvement in the occult, she attended a prophetic ministry campaign led by the prophet Emmanuel Eni. She didn't have the courage to go forward for prayer at the service but went to Eni at night, confessed her sins, and received a prophetic calling to ministry. Not long afterward, she had a nine-hour vision that confirmed her prophetic gift; she heard God say, "I chose Mary because she was God-fearing and humble. Because you are obedient and humble, I will send you to restore my church. . . . Africa shall be saved!" Margaret then began preaching, prophesying, healing, and delivering people from demons around the continent of Africa and became a highly visible and wonderfully humble prophet for Jesus. She is also a Pentecostal bishop and leader of a church of five thousand. Bishop Wanjiru's Jesus Is Alive Ministries has a radio and television program, a magazine, a Web site, and ultramodern facilities.[10] She gained wide respect when she ministered to the victims of the 1998 terrorist bombings in Nairobi.

Another dramatic story of the power of prophetic revelation is that of Simeon Kayiwa of Uganda. Simeon was a philosophy major at Makerere University in Kampala the year President Idi Amin, the brutal dictator, assassinated the Anglican bishop Jana Luwum. Simeon, an atheist at the time, says that Jesus appeared directly in front of him while he was in bed and said, "Wake up! Read Isaiah 60. Go and bring My people back to me. Tell them I am the greatest power in all heaven and earth. Tell them to leave witchcraft and come back to Me. I will be with you to perform miracles and wonders by which people will know that I sent you." Kayiwa told other young people of his vision, and they organized an illegal church that emphasized prophecy, healings, exorcisms, and miracles in the midst of Idi Amin's reign of terror. Reverend Kayiwa's work, which he began as a twenty-year-old college student, is credited with birthing, sustaining, and growing 90 percent of the thirty-five thousand churches in Uganda. The prophet Joel prophesied, and Saint Peter preached, that "your young people will see visions," and Simeon Kayiwa's youthful vision has led to six million more Pentecostal Christians.[11]

Pentecostals tend to move fluidly among prophetically insightful messages, visions, healings, and miracles. They see them all as signs that Jesus is the son of God and the wonders that amaze are intended to confirm the message. They can also carry significant social, cultural, or ethical messages, as in one instance with my parents. Both of my very compassionate and deeply spiritual parents grew up in Pentecostal homes, and all four of my grandparents are Pentecostals. But the prevailing racial prejudices in America still affected them and me. We loved Jesus, supported missionaries around the world, and prayed regularly, but I was nevertheless raised with prejudice against all kinds of racial and ethnic groups. My mother, however, never expressed the racism that affected the rest of us. I found out only recently why that was so. While on a trip to New Mexico at the age of twenty-six, my mom had a vivid vision (only one of three in her life) that she saw in the sky. As she tells it, "I saw a vision of a rainbow. The most unusual thing: it was a circle. God showed me that he wants to include everything, everybody, and don't you *dare* leave anybody out. God was saying, 'You think you've seen a rainbow? I have a real rainbow—it's a complete circle. Every single hue is to be appreciated and loved; it represents my people in the world—every race, every culture—and they all belong together.'"[12]

I have to testify at this point because of the way this story came to my attention. While I was writing this particular chapter, Mom called me one Sunday morning to ask me to pray for my grandma, who has pancreatic cancer. She also told me of a vision she had just a couple of years ago, one with water gushing and flowing from the top of a hill, and how she thinks that relates to Grandma's situation. We prayed for Grandma and the family and talked for a while. But I was a little surprised that my mom was telling me about a vision when, completely unbeknown to her, I was writing a chapter on Pentecostal visions. So I asked her if she'd had others, and she shared the other two she'd had, including the one about the rainbow, acceptance, and reconciliation. She finished by saying, "The Lord is doing marvelous things. Visions are few and far between, but when one comes, I understand why Joseph couldn't keep it to himself. You can't get away from it—is it a vision or a real strong prophetic dream? I don't know, but when we get desperate and say, 'I need a word,' God will move for us. The Holy Ghost moves."

My mother's rainbow vision helped explain to me why she never used racial slurs and tried to keep them to a minimum in our home. The Christianity I was raised in wasn't able to break out very well from the sordid legacy of American racism; that has only happened in fits and starts, and much work remains to be done, but the Spirit was at work in my mom through the vision of all races and cultures coming together as God's people.

Prophecy, Visions, and Dreams in the Bible

Pentecostals, like many other Christians, take their cues from the Bible. But the Bible shows that people can also receive revelations directly from God. Pentecostals are distinctive because they believe and expect that this happens. Mia Sherwood explains her calling to prophetic dream ministry in two sentences: "I said, 'God, how do I know for sure if dreams are from you?' God said, 'Read the Bible.'"[13] Pentecostals read and listen to the Bible and believe it. They believe that the patterns for what they do and believe are found there, that the stories in the Bible are like their stories.

The biblical Joseph is such a famous dreamer that DreamWorks made a movie about him, *Joseph: King of Dreams*.[14] First, he dreamed that eleven sheaves of wheat bowed down to him and that the sun, moon, and eleven stars bowed down to him. He told his eleven brothers this, and it did not go over well; they sold him into slavery in Egypt. He ended up in prison, accused of rape, and interpreted the dreams of his jail mates. One of them, the king's cupbearer, dreamed that he took ripened grapes, squeezed them into the king's cup, and gave the cup to the king. Joseph said that meant that he would be restored to his position as royal cupbearer. The king's baker, emboldened by this interpretation, shared his dream of having on his head three baskets of baked goods for the king, but birds were eating the bread out of the baskets. Joseph said, "The three baskets are three days. Within three days, Pharaoh will lift off your head and hang you on a tree. And the birds will eat away your flesh."[15] Both interpretations proved true.

Two years later, Pharaoh had two dreams. In one dream, seven ugly, skinny cows ate seven sleek, fat cows. In the next one, seven thin, scorched heads of grain swallowed up seven healthy, good heads of grain. None of his magicians or wise men could interpret the dream, but then the cupbearer remembered Joseph in the dungeon, and Joseph was brought before Pharaoh. Joseph humbly told Pharaoh, "I cannot do it, but God will give Pharaoh the answer he desires." Joseph then explained that the two dreams meant the same thing—seven years of abundance would be followed by seven years of drought and famine. He recommended that Pharaoh appoint a discerning and wise person to organize the gathering of a fifth of each year's harvest for seven years so that when the famine followed, Egypt would survive. Pharaoh and his officials thought this was quite wise, and Pharaoh said, "Can we find anyone like this man, one in whom is the Spirit of God? Since God has made all this known to you, there is not one so discerning and wise as you. You shall be in charge of my palace, and all my people are to submit to your orders. Only with respect to the throne will I be greater than you."[16] Joseph's plan worked; Egypt became stronger than ever, the only nation with food during the seven-year drought. And that's what brought Joseph's eleven brothers to Egypt to bow down before him and ask for food. They didn't recognize him, but Joseph recognized them. After planting stolen silver in their grain sacks and scaring them for several months, Joseph finally revealed himself, and they were all reconciled. The entire family then moved to Egypt.

In this story, the Spirit of God helped Joseph interpret the dreams, and Joseph gave God the credit. The work of the Spirit is often linked explicitly to divine revelations like this. Acts 2, the script for Pentecostal faithfulness, has Peter proclaiming that all kinds of people will hear from God through dreams, visions, and prophecies. Saint Peter himself, like my mom and her rainbow, had his own vision directly from God that opened him up to new possibilities in racial and ethnic relationships and made it possible for this new faith to spread beyond the Jewish people.

As a good Jewish man, Peter followed strict dietary rules that prohibited him from eating pigs and all other creatures declared unclean in scripture. But one day while praying on his roof, he had a vision that changed all that. He saw a large sheet descend from heaven that held animals and birds that Jews never ate. Peter heard a voice that said, in effect, "Eat the pig!" Peter responded indignantly, "No way, Lord! I have *never* eaten anything impure or unclean!"[17] The voice said, "Don't you dare call anything impure that God has made clean." This happened three times to make sure Peter got the message: Peter, eat the pig. Peter, eat the pig. Peter, eat the pig. Right after that, while Peter was wondering what the vision could possibly mean, the Spirit told Peter to go downstairs because some Gentiles (non-Jews, and hence considered unclean people) were looking for him. Peter went with them to a Roman soldier's house and explained that he would never have come if it hadn't been for that vision from God. Peter's insight is worth quoting at length, because visions aren't just interesting—they're revolutionary and life-changing. "You are well aware that it is against our law for a Jew to associate with a Gentile or visit him. But God has shown me that I should not call any person impure or unclean. So when I was sent for, I came without raising any objection. . . . I now realize how true it is that God does not show favoritism but accepts people from every nation who respect him and do what is right."

While Peter was speaking, the Holy Spirit came on all of them, and even the Gentiles were filled with the Spirit and spoke in tongues, praising God. Peter's vision from God led to greater racial and ethnic inclusiveness in the early church, but his fellow believers at that point denounced him for eating pig with the Gentiles. Peter told them of his vision and testified that even those pig-eating heathens were filled with the Holy Spirit and spoke in tongues just like he did on Pentecost! He concluded his case by saying, "So if God gave them the same gift as he gave us, who believed in the Lord Jesus Christ, who was I to think that I could oppose God?" At this the entire assembly ceased raising objections, accepted it as a work of the Spirit, and praised God: "So then, God has granted even the Gentiles repentance unto life."[18]

Notice how visions, confession of historical racial prejudices, antiracism initiatives of the Spirit, and speaking in tongues all go together in this story. Pentecostals affirm and open themselves up to these kinds of world-transforming visions. A Jew eating pork with a Gentile because God says it's OK is history-changing—an entire new religion was born from experiences like that.

The Worm in the Apple

One problem with believing that God speaks through prophecies, dreams, and visions is that people can just make stuff up and claim they heard it from God to enhance their own status and further their own agendas. But any religion has its problems with people who co-opt God's name for their own purposes. Sermons can be used in the same selfish ways.

Both Pentecostals and scripture deal with this very real problem by teaching that care should be taken before accepting the message or advice offered by any person—even if the person claims to have seen it in a vision. Matters are settled best with several witnesses, and wisdom leads Pentecostals to take anything they hear with a grain of salt. They fall between the extremes of believing that God no longer reveals anything at all, as some Christians believe, and believing every Christian who says he or she is speaking for God. This classic all-or-nothing approach is applied to dreams, visions, and prophecy; Pentecostals reject both extremes—the all (everyone who has a word should be believed) and the nothing (God doesn't do that, so everybody is wrong). Instead, they try to find a moderate middle ground that is firmly based on the belief that God does indeed still speak through dreams, visions, and prophecies but that each one should be considered and weighed carefully. It's best to talk to friends and family about it, pray about it, and think about it. Reason doesn't fly out the window when God speaks.

What's the Appeal?

For Pentecostals, the belief that God still speaks today and that we can hear God's voice is very helpful; life can get complicated and difficult sometimes. Saint James said, "If anyone needs wisdom, ask of God, who gives liberally and doesn't hold back."[19] The wisdom we often need from God doesn't necessarily come to us in a booming audible voice; it may just be a dream we have at the end of an exhausting day. It may be in the words of a friend or the contemplative prayer of a pastor.

Prophecy, visions, and dreams are appealing because they mean that God has something to say about the state of the world at large and also about the seemingly less significant events in our daily lives. God cares and communicates with us, and that is a reassuring reality to live in. They also mean that God is not limited to working only through rich, powerful, or highly educated people—God can speak to anyone who is listening, and those who listen can then relay God's message to their friends and the rest of the world. God doesn't have the human biases against the less financially well off, the politically disenfranchised, and the non-college-educated. God knows, and Pentecostals know, that anyone is eligible to prophesy, dream, and see visions that are life-transforming. This radical democratization of the Spirit means that God is the ultimate equal opportunity employer—God will employ anyone willing to hear and see what the Spirit is saying and doing.

This means we can admit that sometimes we don't see what we need to be seeing, and we can trust God to enhance or even correct our sight. For instance, a Pentecostal pastor in Singapore learned that his Christianity was not quite what God wanted after he told a father that he would not pray for the healing of the man's child unless the father became a Christian. That night, the pastor had a revelation directly from God as he tossed and turned and could not sleep: "The Holy Spirit told me in no uncertain terms that it was wrong to associate God's love with any conditions." The very next day, he had lunch with the father and apologized. "I have wronged you by telling you God will only heal your son if you become a Christian. I want to tell you today, God will hear you, heal your son, and listen to you because he loves you."[20]

Sometimes it takes a dream or a vision or a prophecy to get us on track. Other times what we are seeing and thinking is confirmed, and that extra bit of confirmation makes all the difference, enabling us to act and live the way we should. Pentecostals live in a world where God can be relied on to communicate, even when it messes up a good night's sleep, so that they can then rest assured that divine guidance and wisdom are lighting their paths.

CHAPTER 8

HOPE, JOY, AND EMOTION

> The joy of the Lord is your strength!
>
> —*Nehemiah 8:10*

Think of something that makes you happy, because this is a chapter of smiles. We know that the world is full of misery, yet in the midst of it and while taking it head on, Pentecostals somehow manage to worship and live joyfully and engender hope. They amaze observers and researchers with their joyous worship, genuine warmth, and openness with their emotions and feelings. There really is something going on in Pentecostal communities; it's not easy to pin it down with quantitative research methods, but Pentecostals claim that it's simple—they are full of the Spirit. One sociologist even observed that Pentecostals don't need drugs to achieve ecstasy; they have Jesus![1]

I read the opening sentence of this chapter to my wife, and she smiled and said, "That sounds like Harry Potter's magical spell *Expecto patronum!*" I didn't understand, so she explained that when there is danger of an attack from a death-dealing Dementor, Harry (and others) can conjure up their deepest happy thought—their joy, their hope, their desire to survive—and say *Expecto patronum!* This innermost positive hope and joy in life then manifests physically in front of them and wards off the destroying enemy that sought to obliterate them. *Expecto patronum* is Latin for "I await a protector" or "I expect

131

something good to happen," and that certainly does sound Pentecostal. Oral Roberts, the Pentecostal televangelist, taught his audience to "expect a miracle," and that's what he titled his autobiography.[2] Positive expectation of good is a hallmark of Pentecostalism.

This positive approach to life is audacious, as in Barack Obama's *Audacity of Hope*. It is rampant throughout the Pentecostal movement and quite contagious. One of the best descriptions of this aspect of the Pentecostal movement is by a Catholic freelance writer who visited a Pentecostal church in Saint Louis, Missouri. She left with great appreciation for her own Catholic theology and rationality and with no intention of changing faiths, yet her observations are worth quoting at length:

> Five women stand on the altar, singing and swaying. One hops up and down, her smile so wide I can't help but smile back. I glance sidelong at the rest of the congregation. Sure enough, I'm the only white chick here. Nobody's staring, though. A comfortable-looking woman walks over to ask the man next to me if he has an aspirin, and as she passes, she squeezes my arm. My heart stops racing. . . . They dance in their pew, jiggling and bopping, throwing their heads back, laughing out loud. They are Pentecostals cutting loose, praising God with the exuberant joy that is their tradition's trademark, and I am jealous. When have I ever felt that free in the house of the Lord? When, for that matter, have I had such fun at Mass? Happy music whirls through this former high school assembly room like a benevolent tornado, picking it right up off the ground and spiraling it closer, closer to God. Grandmothers stay seated but clap to the rock beat—no generation gap here. No one's a stranger, either. Within minutes I have forgotten that I am white, forgotten that I can't dance, forgotten to worry. My body moves of its own accord, carried along by rhythms instinctive and sure, instead of the hesitant, jerky moves I'd expect. I remember my friend Sandy, sister of the pastor, telling me how she first spoke in tongues, how the words rushed forth

without conscious bidding, filling her with joy. . . . The energy of prayer lights up her spirit. Me, I read and analyze and reflect, recite and kneel and imagine and memorize the order of the gestures. . . . I try to imagine a feeling as uninhibited as the worshipers around me, free to dance in the spirit, shout out loud, babble holy nonsense. I burst out laughing—not because I can imagine it but because what comes to mind are the years of near-vicious churchwide arguments over whether to kneel or stand at various points in the liturgy. We're nowhere near a Pentecostal joy.[3]

That's really how it feels. Rosie Zayas, a Pentecostal pastor in Arizona, asks, "Why should we have to be orderly and constrained in church? In Pentecostalism I found self-expression and fellowship. . . . Everyone is so happy."[4] The reporter who interviewed Rosie described the church as full of "emotional shouting, clapping and ecstatic praying" and noted that "Pentecostalism is filled with visible emotion." Pentecostals themselves are fully aware of this; another pastor smiled knowingly as he explained, "People are tired of dry religion. They are looking for a relationship." One of his parishioners testified, "I came to this church to have a relationship with Christ when I had some hard family issues. Now there is a lot of hope."[5]

Statistics from around the globe show that Catholics are switching to Pentecostalism in droves.[6] I know some Pentecostals who have become Catholic, so it's not all one-way traffic, but it's not hard to find published concerns from Catholic leaders or articles with titles like "A Populist Threat Confronts the Catholic Church."[7] One Roman Catholic official describes it this way: "Definitely there is a concern. The thing is that in the Catholic Church, everything is usually very subdued, like the pomp and circumstance and the liturgy. Those Pentecostal churches have more of an emotional thing. It gets you going and appeals to people's feelings."[8]

A leading Hispanic Pentecostal, hopefully a little tongue-in-cheek, says, "We Hispanics are emotional people. We are *telenovela*,

Ricky Martin, J-Lo, salsa and *habañero chiles*. We are fireballs, and here is this religion that is fireball. It engages emotions."[9]

When you open up to emotional relationships with God and others, this can bring hope. You start to feel differently about yourself and the world; once that happens, your actions change, and life can get better. When life gets better, there is true joy! Like a relationship with a lover, the more emotionally vulnerable you are to God, the deeper the relationship. Openness between a husband and a wife creates depth, and deep feelings affect our actions. When I *feel* good about my relationship with my wife, I am a better husband. I think of her more often and remember the little things—like calling her randomly to tell her I love her and remembering not to put the plastic chopsticks in the dishwasher (the most recent dumb thing I've done). This is true with spirituality too—*feeling* good about God or church is more than a belief or thinking that God is good or church is important. Pentecostalism includes emotions as well as intellect and beliefs; it causes people to feel good.

"Belief counts for a lot, but belief isn't enough. For people to take action, they have to *care*."[10] Feelings inspire people to care; with that in mind, some social scientists set out to find out how much difference emotion really makes. They had people fill out surveys and then gave them five $1 bills as compensation. But with the money came an envelope and an invitation to donate to Save the Children, a charity that helps kids around the world. The researchers tested two different approaches to see which generated more generosity, statistics or emotion. Some folks got the potentially heart-wrenching data: three million children in Malawi going hungry; 42 percent drop in maize (corn) production in Zambia, and three million facing severe hunger; eleven million in Ethiopia needing immediate food assistance. The others got an emotional story about a little girl:

> Any money that you donate will go to Rokia, a seven-year-old girl from Mali, Africa. Rokia is desperately poor and faces the threat of severe hunger or even starvation. Her life will be

changed for the better as a result of your financial gift. With
your support, and the support of other caring sponsors, Save the
Children will work with Rokia's family and other members of
the community to help feed and educate her and provide basic
medical care and hygiene education.[11]

Since you're reading a chapter highlighting emotion, you
know that emotion won out over statistics. But by how much?
The people who had the facts—cold, hard statistics—gave an
average of $1.14. The people whose emotions were engaged
by Rokia's story gave more than twice as much, $2.38! That's
almost half of the $5 they had just earned.

But here is where this story of emotions versus analysis
gets even more interesting and I think relates closely to the
ever-expanding success of Pentecostalism. The researchers
decided to test a third group of people by combining statistics
with the emotional story—wouldn't people give even more
if their emotions were engaged *and* they had the hard stats to
prove the depth of the tragedy? Actually, it worked the other
way. Statistics dampened the effect of the emotional tug, and
this group gave only $1.43—a drop in giving of 40 percent!
Something about calculations and analysis seemed to reduce
people's charity, so the researchers did one final experiment to
show the power of emotion. They started by giving their subjects questions that were unrelated to the request for a donation.
For instance, they asked some to calculate the distance traveled
by an object going at fifty miles per hour for ten minutes. Others
were asked to "write down one word to describe how you feel
when you hear the word *baby*."[12] After these opening questions,
analysis versus feeling, *both* groups were given the letter about
Rokia. Ready for the shocker? Those who were primed with calculation gave 46 percent less than those who were primed with
emotion! This led to the conclusion that "the mere *act of calculation* reduced people's charity. Once we put on our analytical hat, we react to emotional appeals differently. We hinder our
ability to feel."[13]

In their chapter on emotions as a key ingredient of sticky ideas and, I believe, of sticky social movements like Pentecostalism, the Heath brothers conclude with this advice: "How can we make people care about our ideas? We get them to take off their Analytical Hats."[14]

Wearing your analytical hat to a Pentecostal church is like wearing a silk tie to a cowboy steakhouse. There's one right down the road from us in San Dimas, California, called Pinnacle Peak, "Home of the Famous Cowboy Steak." There's a big sign that says, "No Ties Allowed!" When my son was seven, he thought it would be great to go there with a tie on and see what happened. So he put on a blue denim shirt and one of my old blue ties, and in we went for a family dinner. When the waiter came to take our order, Nathan couldn't quite bring himself to look the waiter in the eye, but he was jittery with anticipation. About fifteen minutes later, the cowbells started ringing and someone hollered out, "We got us a tie! What do we do with ties?" Everyone in the restaurant hollered back, "We cut 'em off!" They marched over to the grinning, wide-eyed seven-year-old, who was so excited he was bouncing in his seat, hauled out a huge pair of scissors, cut off his tie, and hung it on the wall for all to see. Nathan was so happy the rest of the night, he could barely stand it. The restaurant explains its policy like this:

> Pinnacle Peak is world renowned for its delicious mesquite broiled steaks, huge portions, and "NO NECKTIES ALLOWED" policy. The tradition began one night when we first opened. A customer (city folk) came into the restaurant wearing (can you imagine?) a suit and tie. Well, we took offense (wanting to keep the atmosphere casual) and told the customer, "Either you take off that tie or we'll cut it off." The customer did not heed and was appalled when we cut off his tie. We proudly hung the tie on the rafter with a business card attached to recognize the customer for the loss of his tie, and so all could see that "NO TIES WOULD BE ALLOWED!" Thus the tradition began.

In upholding this tradition, we have cut off tens of thousands of neckties from unsuspecting customers.[15]

Pentecostals are experts at taking off their analytical hats. In fact, they take off their analytical hats and throw them in the air and then do a little dance on them when they hit the floor. Pentecostals have trampled the analytical hats of tens of millions of unsuspecting visitors; many seem to like it, and a lot end up sticking around.

Pentecostalism is world renowned for its buffet of enthusiastic singing, amazing healings, miracles, and prophecies, and its "NO ANALYTICAL HATS ALLOWED" policy. For if there's one thing critics of the movement agree on, it's that Pentecostals are not analytical enough, and they are way too emotional. Pentecostals have been ridiculed from the beginning of the movement for their "emotionalism," so it's kind of ironic that one of the main criticisms of the movement is also one of the main reasons it is so unbelievably successful. The emotional experience is integrally linked to hope and joy, and observers claim that "a major lure of Pentecostalism is the hope it gives worshipers."[16]

You can go to Pinnacle Peak Steakhouse for the experience and you can also go for the meat. After Nathan had his tie cut off and we all enjoyed the laughter and fun, we also ate some good beef and baked potatoes. You can eat a good steak dinner without a tie on. So does the emotionalism of Pentecostalism have substance to go along with it? Can you joyfully throw your analytical hat in the air and also have concrete, life-changing hope that makes a real difference in the world?

As we've seen, scientists who study these things agree that "the act of calculation reduces people's charity" and that "emotions lead to greater compassion and more action."[17] Of course, many other churches and religions besides Pentecostalism bring joy and hope to people's lives, but if we consider the nearly unanimous observations that Pentecostalism is one of the most emotional faiths, we can see why there is a lot of compassion and action that brings joy and hope and why the movement is still growing so fast.

For example, a sociologist at the University of Southern California ran a study on the most socially active churches in the world. He sent out four hundred letters to religious leaders and experts around the world asking for churches that fit the following criteria: (1) fast-growing (2) in the developing world (3) with active social programs addressing needs in their communities that are (4) self-supporting indigenous movements not dependent on outside contributions.[18] To his shock, 85 percent of the churches nominated were Pentecostal; this completely changed the focus of his study.

Stories of social action and transformation abound among Pentecostals—there is indeed substance to the hope. People are drawn to Pentecostal churches because of the faith's joyous worship and the "enveloping sense of community it offers to newcomers." Pastor Tinouco, a pastor of a Pentecostal church in New York City, elaborates on the substance undergirding the emotion: "The first thing I tell the newcomers is that there are no lambs without a shepherd in our church; no one is a stranger. Our mission is to welcome the immigrant and be his guide and his support. If they need money to pay the rent, we'll raise the money for them. If they need work, we'll find them work. If they need someone to talk to, they can come to me."[19] There are engagement parties and birthday parties that everyone is invited to, along with a myriad of other activities throughout the week. One forty-two-year-old mom says, "I feel whole here. This church is not a place we visit once a week. This church is where we hang around and we share our problems and we celebrate our successes, like we were family."[20] The personal and visceral relationship with God extends to personal and emotional relationships with people as well, and it includes such mundane things as rent checks, jobs, and soap.

Florence Muindi, a Pentecostal in Ethiopia, trained groups of "health evangelists" to improve the well-being of four hundred families who lived in her city's dump.[21] These health evangelists regularly visited these families and helped create more sanitary homes through hygiene education. The families then became more stable, and the work and transformation spread to other communities. Social ministries that "emotional" Pentecostals throughout the world are leading include the following:

1. Mercy ministries (providing food, clothing, shelter)
2. Emergency services (responding to floods, famine, earthquake)
3. Education (providing day care, schools, tuition assistance, countering racism, conflict transformation)
4. Counseling service (helping with addiction, divorce, depression)
5. Medical assistance (establishing health clinics, dental clinics, psychological services)
6. Economic development (providing microenterprise loans, job training, affordable housing)
7. The arts (training in music, dance, drama)
8. Policy change (opposing corruption, monitoring elections, advocating living wage, advocating international cooperation)[22]

The emotion within Pentecostalism also corresponds to higher rates of financial giving and tithing. Pentecostals are more than twice as likely to give at least 10 percent of their income to charity as the average American.[23] But Pentecostals are not toying with people's emotions; our emotions are really us, so if we are emotionally affected and want to give more, that is perfectly OK. For instance, visualize the Jerry Lewis Muscular

Dystrophy Association annual telethon on Labor Day. Every year since 1966, it's been a television event that is emotional, funny, and entertaining as it brings hope and joy to children with muscular dystrophy. It also raised over $65 million in less than twenty-four hours in 2008.[24] We could accuse the MDA of toying with us, but there is substance to the hope—these people are working on a cure for a real problem, and emotion opens people to compassion and giving.

Pentecostals and the Jerry Lewis telethon both do the key emotional things that raise the chances of success, growth, and longevity. As the Heath brothers explain, "We create empathy for specific individuals. We show our ideas are associated with things that people already care about . . . , and we appeal to their identities—not only to the people they are right now but also to the people they would like to be."[25]

Hope, Joy, and Emotion in the Bible

Some say Pentecostalism is an experience looking for a theology, but Pentecostals are quick to point out that the Bible is full of hope, joy, and emotional experiences. God's promise to Israel in Jeremiah 29:11 is often quoted and preached among Pentecostals: "'I know the plans I have for you,' declares the LORD, 'plans to prosper you and not to harm you, plans to give you hope and a future.'" This verse appears on artwork, in nurseries, and in sermons, regularly reminding Pentecostals that their prosperity, hope, and happy future are the plans of God. Scripture abounds with stories of people who had been "without hope and without God in the world" finding hope in Jesus and having their lives turned around.[26] Jesus said it was kind of like trading in all your stuff for the mother of all pearls: "The kingdom of heaven is like a shop owner looking for fine pearls. After finding an extremely valuable one, the owner sells everything to buy that pearl."[27] The Samaritan woman who had been married to five husbands and was living with a man she wasn't married to is one of the many who found the valuable pearl. Jesus befriended her and didn't treat her with contempt; because of that, she joyfully told her friends that she had met the Messiah, and many of them believed. The author of the book of Hebrews recounts a litany of faithful believers whose lives were transformed as they "gained what was promised; shut the mouths of lions, quenched the fury of flames, and escaped the edge of the sword; whose weakness was turned to strength. . . . Women received back their dead, raised to life again."[28] Hope is like water for the dehydrated and food for the famished. Jesus said, "I am the bread of life" and "Whoever drinks the water I give will never thirst again."[29]

Hope is not wishful thinking, like "I hope I win the lottery." Hope is more like confident expectation; things will happen because you believe they are true. I asked my mom what she thinks of Pentecostal hope, and she immediately mentioned the Blessed Hope of Jesus' second coming and a "hope beyond this world." Ninety percent of Pentecostals in the United States believe in "the Rapture of the Church, that is, that before the world comes to an end, the religiously faithful will be saved and taken up to heaven."[30] In Pentecostal circles, this is called the Blessed Hope because Titus tells us, "We wait for the blessed hope—the glorious appearing of our great God and Savior, Jesus Christ."[31] Only 59 percent of other Christians believe in the Rapture, but the Blessed Hope and the belief in life after death with God sustain the lives of Pentecostals around the globe.

But these are both "otherworldly" hopes; what about hope in this world? Mom also quoted Romans: "Tribulations develop patience, patience develops experience, and experience develops hope, and hope makes us not ashamed because the love of God is shed abroad in our hearts by the Holy Spirit."[32] The combination of tribulations and hope show that biblical hope is not naive, shallow, or just for after death. It's a confident expectation that God is with us in our daily lives. Hebrews 7:19 calls this "a better hope."

There are over 240 references to *joy* and another 156 to *rejoice* in the Bible. The related word *praise* occurs more than 350 times. That is a whole lot of joyfulness, and Pentecostals receive it gleefully. Saint Paul showed the Pentecostal mix when he said, "Be joyful in hope."[33] But the combination that I think best describes Pentecostals is Paul's prayer for Christians: "May the God of hope fill you with all joy and peace as you trust in him, so that you may overflow with hope by the power of the Holy Spirit."[34] This is hitting on all the Pentecostal cylinders: *filled* to *overflowing* with the *joy, hope,* and *power* of the *Holy Spirit!* That could be the title of this book.

Jesus compared this discovery to finding hidden treasure: "The kingdom of heaven is like treasure hidden in a field. When a man found it, he hid it again, and then in his joy went and sold all he had and bought that field."[35] This kind of overflowing joy and hope is like actually winning the lottery. Can you imagine how happy you would be if you won $1 million? My brother and I used to love planning what we'd do if we won the Publisher's Clearing House sweepstakes. Our family never bought lottery tickets when we were kids because we were Pentecostal and didn't gamble (my dad said the lottery is a tax on people who can't do math), but we could stamp those stickers on the sweepstakes entry forms and mail them in to the free contests. We hoped we would win and enjoyed thinking about how we would spend all that money. We never did win, but sometimes I get the feeling that Pentecostals feel like they've won the religious lottery. They hit the jackpot when they found Jesus! And the more-than-words-can-express joy and power of the Holy Spirit is in this classic Pentecostal song, "It is joy unspeakable and full of glory." It overflows so much, there are just no words to describe it.

Psalms, the songbook of the Bible, has scores of lyrics like these. "My heart leaps for joy. . . . Shout to God with cries of joy! Shout with joy to God, all the earth! Tell of his works with songs of joy. . . . We are filled with joy."[36] Pentecostals love to turn scripture verses into songs, and one that I heard a lot while growing up was

"The joy of the lord is your strength!" This verse from Nehemiah tells the Israelites not to be sad or mourn but to "eat choice foods and drink sweet drinks and send portions to whoever has nothing prepared, for the day is holy to our Lord."[37] So the people ate, drank, and partied joyfully, even in the midst of difficult times.

A friend of mine went to a Pentecostal conference for women and was encouraged to look up all the stories and people in the Bible who were joyful. The speaker told all the women to think of what they were lacking in their lives and to search for it in scripture, and she used joy as her example. My friend was experiencing a serious depression at the time and shared with me that as she began journaling her way through all the scripture passages related to joy, joyfulness, and rejoicing, she regained her strength and was slowly transformed into a healthier person.

With such hope and joy, how can we not be emotional? But emotions in scripture also include sadness and anger because of injustice and suffering. Jesus cried real tears when his friend Lazarus died, and Peter "went outside and wept bitterly" after denying that he was a follower of Jesus.[38] Jeremiah is called "the weeping prophet" because he was rightfully frustrated about the rampant unfaithfulness in Jerusalem and Israel that led to their destruction. There's even an entire book in the Bible called Lamentations, which is a "song of wailing" in which the prophet mourns despondently. The Bible has the whole range of emotions—from jubilant rejoicing to the depths of despair, and so do Pentecostals. They sometimes confess and repent of their sins with great emotion and sadness, reminiscent of the prophetic calls for repentance issued in the Old Testament. "Put on sackcloth, O priests, and mourn; wail, you who minister before the altar. Come, spend the night in sackcloth."[39]

When I was twenty-two years old, I attended a Pentecostal convention with thousands of others where something like this happened. During the time of prayer before the preaching started, a woman gave a message in tongues that stopped the service in its tracks. Without the aid of a microphone, her voice reached every corner of the auditorium, and the sheer intensity of her emotional appeal—in a language none of us understood—gave me goose bumps. After a short pause, a man went to the front and asked if he could have the microphone because he believed he had the interpretation. Quietly and carefully, but with great emotion, he told the room full of pastors that God was calling us all to repent of our selfishness, our greed, and our materialism. He said that God wants to empower us to serve him, but the Assemblies of God had gotten off track and was deep in sin, and the only way to change course was to humble ourselves and truly, deeply, and completely repent and ask God to forgive us. This interpretation of the message in tongues hit the mark, and people began to cry and pray at their pews and in the altars at the front of the church. I sank to my knees and then lay face-down in the carpet and wept.

This time of repentance and prayer lasted almost an hour; it was a time not of rejoicing or celebration but of introspection and repentance. People had heard the message from God, were thinking about the sin in their own lives, and were confessing and asking for forgiveness. Eventually, the atmosphere among the several thousand people present changed. God's light had shone right into the darkness of our materialism, we had admitted it and committed ourselves to transformation, and we began to feel the weight of our sins lift. As the feeling in the room shifted, the musicians began to play, and we entered into singing that reflected the liberation we were feeling. There is a verse in scripture that expresses what we experienced: "Weeping may endure for a night, but joy comes in the morning."[40] Pentecostals seem to experience and express the extremes found in scripture more intensely and more freely than other faith traditions.

What Are the Problems?

Feelings can let us down, emotions wane, and sometimes we're just not happy. Life is not all mountaintop experiences, but sometimes around Pentecostals you get the idea that it's supposed

to be that way. Sometimes there is an underlying or even bla-
tant attitude that if you're not just bubbling over with giddiness,
there's something wrong with you. The pressure to be happy can
be a huge burden to carry and can create false personas and a culture of fake happiness. Some Pentecostals in the Word of Faith
part of the movement won't admit to feeling sadness or anger
because that is seen to be opening up a foothold for the devil.
This leads people to say things and act in ways that are directly
the opposite of reality. They are trying to speak another reality
into existence by denying what they don't like about how they
really do feel. But all joy and no recognition of suffering does not
square with reality or with the way Christians lived in the Bible.

Deryl, a friend of mine, lost her son in a tragic accident a few
years ago. The people at the Pentecostal church she attended
told her she needed to just quit being sad and rejoice in all the
good that was in her life. I'm not a psychologist, but from my
theological perspective, that was poor advice. She did not need
to look in a mirror with a big, stretchy, stiff grin and just repeat
"I'm happy, I'm happy, I'm happy" until it came true. Not all
Pentecostals would have told her to do this, but it is a potential
problem when joy is such an important part of the ethos of the
movement.

Why didn't the freelance reporter who wished her Catholic
church had even just a smidgeon of Pentecostal joy want to
become Pentecostal? Because she thought that there was no substance to the sermon that followed the emotion. The preacher
seemed "incapable of thinking with depth" regarding political
issues, and he attributed "addictions and neuroses to satanic
influences, and the solution was to drive out demons." She confessed, "I leave hurriedly, upset, missing the earlier fun of the
worship, wondering why intellect and emotion can't ever exist
in equipoise. . . . When we reserve judgment, we also reserve our
emotional expression. I do not regret this. . . . And joy is a small
price to pay for safety."[41] Emotional worship does not have to
be followed by lousy preaching, and lousy preaching can follow
hopeless, joyless, emotionless worship, too. But we can get

addicted to emotion and may not realize how little depth we have—like pop culture that cranks out media that titillates and entertains but doesn't say anything worth remembering. Even a seven-year-old will enjoy getting his tie cut off just the first few times. Eventually, he will be more interested in the steak dinner. The problem with emotionalism is that it can mask a lack of substance and make it harder to reflect.

What's the Appeal?

People like to feel good. It's better than feeling bad. And Pentecostalism helps people feel good. Pentecostalism "gives voice to feelings—the pain, the joy, the hope for new life."[42] After returning from a trip to Africa, Brian McLaren noted that "Pentecostal joy is itself a revolutionary manifestation of the kingdom of God in the land of HIV, Idi Amin, civil war, genocide, and breathtaking poverty."[43] There is a lot more to Africa than all of those negatives, but his observation is powerful. "A revolutionary manifestation of the kingdom of God" is extremely appealing.

The "deprivation theory" explaining the appeal of Pentecostalism says that people who are deprived of the basic necessities of life will be attracted to religions that help them cope with their misery and pain; Pentecostalism is thus only for poor, less educated, possibly addle-brained people. According to this line of thinking, Pentecostalism should work only for the down and out. But although this theory may have some explanatory merit, it is being beaten back and nuanced by those who see Pentecostalism as a social movement that does much more than just attract society's "losers."[44] Pentecostalism flourishes among middle-class, educated, and "normal" people as well; it's success among only the less well positioned is a myth—a typical outsider's understanding of the appeal of Pentecostalism. Deprivation theory's insulting categorization of people hides the fact that something in Pentecostalism appeals to a much wider swath of humanity, and I think a significant piece of the "why's it growing so fast?" puzzle is the emotional freedom it provides.

So I'm going to explain the appeal of Pentecostal joy, hope, and emotion by turning the deprivation theory on its head and humbly suggest that some moneyed, educated, and analytical folks may be deprived of emotional freedom and suffer because of it. They don't suffer in the same ways as a woman living on $1 a day in Bangladesh, but even the well-to-do need a bit of head-clearing catharsis and emotional expression. Harvey Cox, a Harvard researcher, believes that Pentecostalism is so attractive to such a wide range of people because it helps fill the "ecstasy deficit" in our postmodern world.[45] In other words, we as a people have "lost that lovin' feelin'," but Pentecostalism hasn't. He claims that people have had the emotion squeezed out of them by modernity's demand for rationality and that we're looking for a way to be whole again; Pentecostalism is an answer to this problem. Allan Anderson, a Pentecostal professor at the University of Birmingham in England, critiques and nuances that idea by claiming that Pentecostalism's openness to the "freedom of the Spirit" means that it is amazingly able to contextualize itself. By being less rigid and formal and more emotional and open to feeling and context, the Pentecostal spirituality of hope and joy can "enhance an individual's sense of belonging to a community, meet felt needs and bring a greater awareness of and love for both God and one's neighbour."[46] Pentecostalism is appealing because you can actually "feel the love."

Anomie is a sociological term referring to feelings of isolation, alienation, and lack of normalcy owing to changes in society. This sort of social unrest is related to the fact that people move around so much now, from rural areas to the cities and then from city to city and apartment to apartment or home to home. There are fewer norms in the large cities of the world, and loneliness is a real problem. "Employment is often unstable; housing is precarious; and vices, such as gambling, prostitution, drugs, and alcohol, are typically rampant. Within this context, the attraction of Pentecostalism is obvious: it brings order, stability, and hope to people who are living precarious lives."[47] This is real hope, hope like prostitutes in India found when a local Pentecostal church wanted to help them unionize.[48] The church had been buying them out of prostitution, but that only increased the prices being paid to poor families for their girls and compounded the problem, so the Pentecostals changed their strategy. They worked structurally to improve the women's living and working conditions and took care of their children so that the youngsters would not be exposed to the same dangers.

The hope provided by Pentecostalism is appealing because the churches "often function like surrogate extended families."[49] Families take care of one another and celebrate together, and being part of a family is extremely healthy. One study by psychologists at Syracuse University found that family routines, rituals, and celebrations drastically improve "parenting competence, child adjustment, and marital satisfaction."[50] Women are rightfully hopeful when they get involved in Pentecostal churches because "social order prevails" and their family becomes part of "a cohesive, caring community."[51]

People who take on big problems in the world get exhausted, and Pentecostals are trying to save the world. I have a friend who lived in the West Bank working for peace with justice for Israel and Palestine. She is from a mainline Protestant denomination, and nobody ever guessed that she prayed in tongues, but her tough work led her to seek a spirituality that would undergird and strengthen her hope. When she finally admitted publicly that she had a "charismatic spirituality," it surprised her coworkers. She is one of millions of people who are described beautifully in this passage, written by a non-Pentecostal, about Pentecostals engaged in frontline social ministries:

> The work of doing social ministry is not easy; it requires ministering to people who are often sick, despairing, and living on the margins of society. If one is going to assist these individuals,

then one needs *hope*. And, equally important, one needs to transmit this hope to others with a spirit of *joy*. Otherwise, the task becomes dreary and, for many, unsustainable. . . . Pentecostals . . . are filled with new *hope* and desire for a better world. The challenge is to channel these emotions, these feelings, these desires. . . . We have seen a unique quality in many of the people we encountered during our research, which was a residual spirit of *joy*.[52]

Emotional freedom, hopefulness, and joy seem to be as significant as any other factors in explaining why Pentecostalism is such a fast-growing faith. Pentecostals see themselves as people of the Spirit, and as the song says, "Where the Spirit of the Lord is, there is freedom." Freedom to weep, freedom to dance, freedom to celebrate, and freedom to hope for and experience a better life. No wonder it's contagious.

NOTES

Chapter One: Just Ask: A World of Miracles Awaits

1. John 21:25 (author's translation).
2. John 14:12 (AMP and author's paraphrase).
3. Acts 3:6–10, Acts 5:12–16, Acts 20:9–10, James 5:14–15 (NIV).
4. Mark 16:16–18 (NIV).
5. Assemblies of God, "Our Message: Four Truths at the Heart of It All," 2008, http://ag.org/top/Beliefs/Our_Message.cfm#Healing
6. Reinhard Bonnke, *Raised from the Dead* (Full Flame Productions, 2001).
7. Acts 8:39–40, I Kings 18:12 (NIV).
8. Luke 18:1–8 (NIV).
9. Mark 9:24 (NIV).
10. Martin Luther King Jr., "A Christmas Sermon on Peace," in *A Testament of Hope: The Essential Writings and Speeches of Martin Luther King Jr.* (San Francisco: HarperOne, 1991), p. 257.
11. Dale A. Matthews and Connie Clark, *The Faith Factor: Proof of the Healing Power of Prayer* (New York: Penguin, 1999).
12. Pew Forum on Religion and Public Life, *Spirit and Power: A 10-Country Survey of Pentecostals* (Washington, D.C.: Pew Forum on Religion and Public Life, 2006), p. 4.
13. Wonsuk Ma, "Korea," in *Encyclopedia of Pentecostal and Charismatic Christianity*, ed. Stanley Burgess (New York: Routledge, 2006), p. 278. Pat Robertson claims to have seen

a crowd of 1.2 million for a Pentecostal service in India; see CBN.com, "Reinhard Bonnke Tells of Nigerian Man Raised from the Dead," n.d., http://www.cbn.com/700club/features/bonnke_raisedpastor.aspx

14. Pew Forum, *Spirit and Power*, p. 2.

Chapter Two: Worship and Music

1. Pentecostal Place.com, "About," n.d., http://pentecostalplace.wordpress.com/about

2. Donald Miller and Tetsunao Yamamori, *Global Pentecostalism: The New Face of Christian Social Engagement* (Berkeley: University of California Press, 2007), pp. 84–88.

3. Ibid., p. 87.

4. Ephesians 5:18–19 (NIV).

5. Daniel Ramírez, "Migrating Faiths: A Social and Cultural History of Pentecostalism in the U.S.-Mexico Borderlands," doctoral dissertation, Duke University, 2005, p. 319.

6. Jane Lampman, "Pentecostalism at 100: A Major Religious Force," *Christian Science Monitor*, Apr. 25, 2006, http://www.csmonitor.com/2006/0424/p01s01-lire.html

7. Telford Work, "Tradition 102: Charismatic Workshop," lecture at Westmont College, Nov. 8, 2000, http://www.westmont.edu/~work/lectures/charismaticchapel.html

8. David Daniels III in "Pentecostal Addresses NCC General Assembly, Marking a First," National Council of Churches, Nov. 11, 1998, http://www.ncccusa.org/98ga/pent.html

9. Steven Feld, *Sound and Sentiment: Birds, Weeping, Poetics, and Song in Kaluli Expression* (Philadelphia: University of Pennsylvania Press, 1982). Cited in Ramírez, "Migrating Faiths," p. 306.

10. 2 Samuel 6:21 (NIV).

11. 2 Samuel 6:16 (NIV).

12. Tyler Cowen, "What Makes a Country Wealthy? Maybe It's the Working Stiff," *New York Times*, Nov. 2, 2006, http://www.nytimes.com/2006/11/02/business/02scene.html?pagewanted=print

13. Tex Sample, *White Soul: Country Music, the Church, and Working Americans* (Nashville, Tenn.: Abingdon Press, 1996).

14. Ibid., p. 29.

15. Ibid., p. 31.

16. Ibid., p. 30.

17. Ibid., p. 31.

18. Bob McDill, Wayland Holyfield, and Chuck Neese, "Rednecks, White Socks, and Blue Ribbon Beer" (Copyright 1973 Jack Music, Inc., and Jando Music, Inc.).

19. Sample, *White Soul*, p. 32.

20. Ibid., pp. 32–33.

21. Ibid., p. xx.

22. Mark A. Kellner, "Flock Strays from U.S. Churches," *Washington Times*, Oct. 18, 2002.

23. Sample, *White Soul*, p. 39.

24. Manuel H. Peña, *The Texas-Mexican Conjunto: History of a Working-Class Music* (Austin, Tex.: University of Austin Press, 1985), p. 242.

25. Ramírez, "Migrating Faiths," p. 319.

26. Sample, *White Soul*, p. 50.

27. Ibid., p. 63.

28. Ibid., p. xx.

29. Richard Hoggart, *The Uses of Literacy* (New Brunswick, N.J.: Transaction, 1991), pp. 120, 238.

30. David Ruis, "Every Move I Make" (Copyright 1996 Vineyard Music).

31. Sample, *White Soul*, p. 74.

32. Ibid., p. xx.

33. Richard Black, "Enemy's Camp" (Copyright 1991 Sound III, Inc.).

34. Sample, *White Soul*, p. 76.

35. Ibid., p. 77.
36. Ramírez, "Migrating Faiths," p. 272.
37. Ibid., p. 276.
38. Vernon M. McCombs, *From Over the Border: A Study of the Mexicans in the United States* (New York: Council of Women for Home Missions, 1925), p. 86.
39. Ramírez, "Migrating Faiths," p. 285.
40. Ibid., pp. 290, 291, 293.
41. Ibid., p. 295.
42. Ibid., p. 294.
43. Ibid., p. 300.
44. Ibid., p. 285.
45. James R. Goff Jr., "Conflicted by the Spirit: The Religious Life of Elvis Presley," *Assemblies of God Heritage*, 2008, 28, 22–31.
46. Alyn Shipton, *A New History of Jazz*, 2nd. ed. (New York: Continuum, 2007), pp. 4–5.
47. Ken Burns, *Jazz: A Film by Ken Burns*, episode 2: "The Gift" (Florentine Video/PBS Home Video/Warner Home Video, 2000).
48. Ibid.
49. Ibid.
50. Eric Hobsbawm, *The Jazz Scene* (New York: Pantheon, 1993), p. 229. (Originally published 1959)
51. Ibid., pp. 230–232.
52. Ibid., p. 233.
53. Ibid., p. 239. In 1996, Harvey Cox wrote, "In recent years I have heard some of the finest jazz improvisations and chordal innovations to be found anywhere in Pentecostal churches, and I have come to believe that there is a special kinship between the religion that was born in America and the music that was born here too, between Pentecostalism and jazz." Harvey Cox, *Fire from Heaven: The Rise of Pentecostal Spirituality and the Reshaping of Religion in the Twenty-First Century* (Boston: Addison-Wesley, 1996), p. 143.
54. Hobsbawm, *Jazz Scene*, p. 245.

Chapter Three: Tongue-Talking

1. Classical Pentecostals "belong either to one of the historical Pentecostal denominations, such as the Assemblies of
God and the Church of God in Christ, that have their
roots in the American religious revivals of the early 20th
century, or to newer, largely independent indigenous
churches." Charismatics "share many of the experiences
that are distinctive to Pentecostalism but remain members
of mainstream Protestant [Methodist, Baptist, Lutheran,
Presbyterian, Episcopalian, and others], Catholic, and
Orthodox denominations." Pew Forum on Religion and
Public Life, *Spirit and Power: A 10-Country Survey of
Pentecostals* (Washington, D.C.: Pew Forum on Religion
and Public Life, 2006), pp. iv–v. Furthermore, in the United
States, "18% of Charismatics are classified as such solely
because they describe themselves as Charismatic Christians;
15% of Charismatics qualify solely because they describe
themselves as Pentecostal Christians but do not belong to
explicitly Pentecostal denominations; 43% of Charismatics
are classified as such solely because they say they speak in
tongues; and the remaining 24% of U.S. Charismatics qualify as such by multiple measures." Pew Forum, *Spirit and
Power*, p. 3.
2. This person's identity has been changed at her request, but
the story is accurate and is presented with her permission.
3. "Weird Babble of Tongues," *Los Angeles Times*, Apr. 18, 1906, p. 1.
4. Romans 8:26 (NIV).
5. Norman Maclean (author) and Richard Friedenbert (screen-
play), *A River Runs Through It* (Allied Filmmakers, 1992).
6. Margaret M. Poloma, "Glossolalia, Liminality, and Empowered
Kingdom Building: A Sociological Perspective," in Mark J.
Cartledge, ed., *Speaking in Tongues: Multi-Disciplinary Perspectives*
(Milton Keynes, England: Paternoster, 2006), pp. 157, 167, 171.
7. Acts 2:1–4 (author's translation).

8. Acts 2:38–39 (*The Message*; author's translation).
9. 1 Corinthians 14:18 (NIV).
10. Acts 10:44–46 (NIV; author's translation).
11. Acts 11:15–17 (NIV; author's translation).
12. 1 Corinthians 12:22–24 (NIV).
13. 1 Corinthians 13:4–8 (NIV; NASB).
14. 1 Corinthians 12:30–13:1 (NIV; NASB).
15. 1 Corinthians 12:1; 13:13–14:4 (NIV; NASB; author's translation).
16. 1 Corinthians 14:6–12 (NIV).
17. 1 Corinthians 14:19 (NIV).
18. 1 Corinthians 14:23 (NIV; author's translation).
19. 1 Corinthians 14:25, 28 (NIV).
20. 1 Corinthians 14:39–40 (*The Message*; NIV).
21. Poloma, "Glossolalia," pp. 168–169.
22. James K. A. Smith, "Tongues as 'Resistance Discourse': A Philosophical Perspective," in Cartledge, *Speaking in Tongues*, p. 93.
23. Poloma, "Glossolalia," p. 168.
24. Smith, who himself prays in tongues, calls himself a Charismatic rather than a Pentecostal because he does not believe "that tongues is the initial and only physical evidence of the baptism in the Holy Spirit."
25. Smith, "Tongues as 'Resistance Discourse,'" p. 161.
26. Ibid., p. 169.
27. Ibid., pp. 170–171.

Chapter Four: Prosperity (or Money, Money, Money, Money)

1. Deji Isaac Ayegboyin, "A Rethinking of Prosperity Teaching in the New Pentecostal Churches in Nigeria," *Black Theology*, 2006, 4, 81.
2. Brett Shipp, "Jet Flight Records Spur Copeland Ministry Questions," *Dallas Morning News*, Feb. 28, 2007; Eric Gorski, "Wealth of Minister Kenneth Copeland and Family Scrutinized," *Lakeland* (Fla.) *Ledger*, July 28, 2008.

3. Norman Vincent Peale, http://normanvincentpeale.wwwhubs.com

4. Gloria Copeland, *God's Will Is Prosperity* (Fort Worth, Tex.: Kenneth Copeland Ministries, 1987).

5. Kenneth Copeland and Leroy Thompson, http://pulpit-pimps. org/audio/copeland/Kenny-and-Leroy-silliness.MP3

6. Ron Sider, *Rich Christians in an Age of Hunger* (Nashville, Tenn.: Nelson, 1977).

7. Pew Forum on Religion and Public Life, *Spirit and Power: A 10-Country Survey of Pentecostals* (Washington, D.C.: Pew Forum on Religion and Public Life, 2006), p. 29.

8. Malachi 3:10–12 (NIV).

9. Michael Okonkwo, *Controlling Wealth God's Way*; quoted in Isaac Phiri and Joe Maxwell, "Gospel Riches," *Christianity Today*, July 2007, p. 2.

10. Lawrence Nwankwo, "Reviewing the Prosperity Message in the Light of a Theology of Empowerment," *Journal of the European Pentecostal Theological Association*, 2002, 22, 59–60.

11. Pew Forum, *Spirit and Power*, p. 54.

12. Ibid.

13. Nwankwo, "Reviewing the Prosperity Message," p. 61.

14. Stephen Buckley, "Prosperity Theology Pulls on Purse Strings: Promises of Riches Entice Brazil's Poor," *Washington Post Foreign Service*, Feb. 13, 2001, p. 1.

15. Ziva Branstetter, "Robert Tilton: From Downfall to Windfall, Living on a Prayer," *Tulsa World*, May 4, 2003, http://www. trinityfi.org/press/tulsaworld02.html

16. Ibid.

17. Ibid.

18. Success N Life (Robert Tilton's Web site), Feb. 1, 2008, http://www.successinlife.tv/tiltonmaterial.html

19. Assemblies of God, "The Believer and Positive Confession," Jan. 31, 2008, http://www.ag.org/top/Beliefs/Position_Papers/ pp_4183_confession.cfm

20. Stephen Strang, "Benny Hinn Speaks Out," *Charisma*, Aug. 1993, pp. 26–28.

21. Proverbs 30:8–9 (NIV).

22. Bruce Wilkinson, *The Prayer of Jabez: Breaking Through to the Blessed Life* (Sisters, Ore.: Multnomah Books, 2000), p. 13.

23. Buckley, "Prosperity Theology," p. 2.

24. WordNet Search 3.0, "Poverty," Nov. 12, 2008, http://wordnet. princeton.edu/perl/webwn; A Dollar a Day: Finding Solutions to Poverty, "Glossary of Poverty-Related Terms, 2006, http://library.thinkquest.org/05aug/00282/other_glossary.htm

25. Arlene Sanchez Walsh, "First Church of *Prosperidad*," *Christianity Today*, July 2007, p. 31.

26. Pew Forum, *Spirit and Power*, p. 51.

27. British Broadcasting Corporation, "Gap Pulls 'Child Labour' Clothing," Oct. 28, 2007, http://news.bbc.co.uk/2/hi/south_asia/7066019.stm

28. Luke 6:17 (NIV).

29. Assemblies of God, "Believer and Positive Confession."

30. Ayegboyin, "Rethinking of Prosperity Teaching," p. 72.

31. Donald Miller and Tetsunao Yamamori, *Global Pentecostalism: The New Face of Christian Social Engagement* (Berkeley: University of California Press, 2007), p. 177.

32. Ibid., pp. 42–43.

33. Acts 2:42–47, 4:32–37, 6:1–7 (NIV).

34. Ben Woolsey and Matt Schulz, "Credit Card Industry Facts, Debt Statistics, 2006–2008," Credit Cards.com, Oct. 22, 2008, http://www.creditcards.com/statistics/credit-card-industry-facts-personal-debt-statistics-1276.php

35. Dave Ramsey, "The Truth About Credit Card Debt," 2008, http://www.daveramsey.com/the_truth_about/%20credit_card_debt_3478.html.cfm

36. Ellen Graham, "Southern Pastor Works to Deliver His Flock from Credit-Card Debt," *Wall Street Journal*, June 12, 2002, http://www.goodsenseministry.com/forum/articledetail.asp?artID=16

37. Lisa Armstrong, "Forgive Us Our Debts: Mount Carmel Baptist Church Is Teaching Its Congregation How to

Manage Credit," *Black Enterprise*, Nov. 1, 2002, http://
findarticles.com/p/articles/mi_m1365/is_4_33/ai_93307087/
pg_1?tag=artBody;col1
38. Graham, "Southern Pastor."
39. Acts 2:44–47, 4:32–34 (NIV).
40. Graham, "Southern Pastor."
41. Ibid.

Chapter Five: Storytelling

1. Stanley Hauerwas, *Christian Existence Today: Essays on Church, World, and Living in Between* (Grand Rapids, Mich.: Baker, 1995), p. 28.
2. Stanley Hauerwas, *The Peaceable Kingdom* (Notre Dame, Ind.: University of Notre Dame Press, 1983), p. 25; Jean Bethke Elshtain, "Christian Contrarian," CNN.com, 2001, http://www.cnn.com/SPECIALS/2001/americasbest/TIME/society.culture/pro.shauerwas.html
3. Hauerwas, *Peaceable Kingdom*, p. 27.
4. Ibid., p. 29.
5. Ibid., p. 36.
6. Hauerwas, *Christian Existence Today*, p. 102.
7. Hauerwas, *Peaceable Kingdom*, p. 30.
8. Luke 7:18–35 (NIV).
9. John 14:12–13 (author's paraphrase).
10. From my journal entry on June 10, 1992.
11. From my journal entry on June 17, 1992. Acts 9:32–35 (TNIV) reads, "As Peter traveled about the country, he went to visit the Lord's people who lived in Lydda. There he found a man named Aeneas, who was paralyzed and had been bedridden for eight years. 'Aeneas,' Peter said to him, 'Jesus Christ heals you. Get up and roll up your mat.' Immediately, Aeneas got up. All those who lived in Lydda and Sharon saw him and turned to the Lord."
12. An undated entry in my journal from the summer of 1992.

13. From my journal entry on July 3, 1992.

14. Jon Trott and Mike Hertenstein, "Selling Satan: The Tragic History of Mike Warnke," *Cornerstone Magazine*, 1992, *21*, http://www.cornerstonemag.com/features/iss098/warnke_index.htm

15. Mike Warnke, *The Satan Seller* (South Plainfield, N.J.: Bridge, 1972).

16. Myung Soo Park, "Korean Pentecostal Spirituality as Manifested in the Testimonies of Believers of the Yoido Full Gospel Church," *Asian Journal of Pentecostal Studies*, 2004, *7*, 43.

17. Phillip Jenkins, *The New Faces of Christianity: Believing the Bible in the Global South* (Oxford: Oxford University Press, 2006), p. 112.

18. Ibid., p. 113.

19. Acts 6:8–8:1; 9:1–26; 22.

20. Transcribed from a Joel Osteen sermon on YouTube, http://www.youtube.com/watch?v=sw6DTOhGgrU

21. Martin Olausson, "The Television and Movie Industry Explained: Where Does All the Money Go?" Strategy Analytics, June 8, 2007, http://www.strategyanalytics.com/default.aspx?mod=ReportAbstractViewer&a0=3462

22. Norman Herr, "Television and Health," Internet Resources to Accompany *The Sourcebook for Teaching Science*, California State University, Northridge, 2007, http://www.csun.edu/science/health/docs/tv&health.html

23. NationMaster.com, "Films Produced (Most Recent) by Country, 2003, http://www.nationmaster.com/graph/med_fil_pro-media-films-produced

24. Chip Heath and Dan Heath, *Made to Stick: Why Some Ideas Survive and Others Die* (New York: Random House, 2007).

25. Deborah A. Small, George Lowenstein, and Paul Slovic, "Can Insight Breed Callousness? The Impact of Learning About the Identifiable Victim Effect on Sympathy," working paper, University of Pennsylvania, 2005. Cited in ibid., pp. 165–169.

26. Save Africa's Children, "Elosy," 2007, http://www.saveafricas
   children.com/site/PageServer?pagename=reality_hope_5_elosy

27. Heath and Heath, *Made to Stick*, p. 214.

Chapter Six: Power and Spiritual Warfare

1. Personal interview; the names have been changed.

2. Personal interview; the names have been changed.

3. Don Rogers, "Territorial Spirits," Spiritual Warfare Ministries
   Online, 1999, http://www.sw-mins.org/strat6.html

4. The Assemblies of God USA officially teaches that spiritual
   warfare and demon activity are real, but they criticize others who they think have pushed it too far. See Assemblies
   of God, "Spiritual Warfare (Attacks of Satan)," n.d., http://
   www.ag.org/top/Beliefs/sptlissues_spiritual_warfare.cfm

5. Ibid.

6. John 10:10 (NASB): "The thief comes only to steal and kill
   and destroy; I come so that they may have life, and have it
   abundantly."

7. 2 Timothy 1:7 (NIV).

8. Myung Soo Park, "Korean Pentecostal Spirituality as Manifested
   in the Testimonies of Believers of the Yoido Full Gospel
   Church," *Asian Journal of Pentecostal Studies*, 2004, 7, 43.

9. Ibid.

10. Nak-hyung Kim, "Faithfulness with All the Heart, Life, and
    Will," *Shinanggye*, July 1976, p. 62.

11. Phillip Jenkins, "The New Faces of Christianity: Believing the
    Bible in the Global South," interview with Joanne J. Myers,
    Oct. 11, 2006, http://www.cceia.org/resources/transcripts/5399.html

12. Ibid.

13. Mark 1:24 (NIV).

14. Allan Anderson, *An Introduction to Pentecostalism: Global
    Charismatic Christianity* (Cambridge: Cambridge University
    Press, 2004), p. 201.

15. Mark 1:27 (NIV, NASB).

16. Mark 5:4–5 (NIV).
17. Mark 5:15 (NIV, NASB).
18. Mark 16:17–18 (NIV).
19. Willard M. Swartley, "Jesus Christ: Victor over Evil," in Ray Gingerich and Ted Grimsrud, eds., *Transforming the Powers: Peace, Justice, and the Domination System* (Minneapolis, Minn.: Fortress, 2006), p. 98.
20. Luke 8:50 (KJV), Matthew 28:20 (NASB).
21. Acts 13:9–10 (NIV).
22. Acts 19:11–20 (NIV).
23. Frank Peretti, *This Present Darkness* (Wheaton, Ill.: Crossway, 1986), p. 36.
24. Ogbu Kalu, *African Pentecostalism: An Introduction* (Oxford: Oxford University Press, 2008), p. 81.
25. See Walter Wink, *Engaging the Powers: Discernment and Resistance in a World of Domination* (Minneapolis, Minn.: Fortress, 1992), pp. 5–7; and Walter Wink, "The New Worldview: Spirit at the Core of Everything," in Gingerich and Grimsrud, *Transforming the Powers*, pp. 21–28.
26. Jenkins, "New Faces of Christianity."
27. Personal interview with Nick Stuva, Aug. 9, 2008.
28. Kalu, *African Pentecostalism*, pp. 80, 175–186.
29. Ibid., pp. 176–179.
30. Ibid., p. 179.
31. Ibid.
32. Ibid., p. 181.
33. Baylor Institute for Studies of Religion, *American Piety in the 21st Century: New Insights into the Depths and Complexity of Religion in the U.S.* (Waco, Tex.: Baylor Institute for Studies of Religion, 2006), p. 20.
34. Pew Forum on Religion and Public Life, *Spirit and Power: A 10-Country Survey of Pentecostals* (Washington, D.C.: Pew Forum on Religion and Public Life, 2006), p. 26.
35. Baylor Institute, *American Piety*, p. 45.
36. Ibid., p. 49.
37. Kalu, *African Pentecostalism*, pp. 89–90.

Chapter Seven: Prophecy, Visions, and Dreams

1. Marlon Millner, "Send Judah First: A Pentecostal Perspective on Peace," Pentecostal Charismatic Peace Fellowship, 2003, http://www.pcpf.org/index.php?option=com_content&task=view&id=261&Itemid=45. Several dozen Pentecostal pastors, students, laity, and teachers signed the letter.

2. Baylor Institute for Studies of Religion, *American Piety in the 21st Century: New Insights into the Depths and Complexity of Religion in the U.S.* (Waco, Tex.: Baylor Institute for Studies of Religion, 2006), p. 45.

3. Ibid., p. 46.

4. Pew Forum on Religion and Public Life, *Spirit and Power: A 10-Country Survey of Pentecostals* (Washington, D.C.: Pew Forum on Religion and Public Life, 2006), p. 17.

5. Mia Sherwood Ministries, http://www.heartsongministry.com. To submit a dream, visit http://groups.yahoo.com/group/propheticdreams

6. Pete Pentecostal, "Prophecy," July 29, 2007, http://petepentecostal.blogspot.com/2007/07/prophecy.html

7. Margaret Poloma, *Main Street Mystics: The Toronto Blessing and Reviving Pentecostalism* (Walnut Creek, Calif.: Altamira Press, 2003), p. 123.

8. Ibid., p. 116.

9. Personal interview with Don Niemyer, Apr. 27 2008.

10. Ogbu Kalu, *African Pentecostalism: An Introduction* (Oxford: Oxford University Press, 2008), pp. 150–151; Phillip Jenkins, *The New Faces of Christianity: Believing the Bible in the Global South* (Oxford: Oxford University Press, 2008), p. 166; Jesus Is Alive Ministries, http://www.jiam.org

11. Kalu, *African Pentecostalism*, p. 96. It is also claimed that Kayiwa has raised eighteen people from the dead.

12. Personal interview with Sharon Alexander, June 29, 2008.

13. Mia Sherwood Ministries, "Academy of Dream Interpretation," n.d., http://www.heartsongministry.com/dream_academy.html

14. Rob LaDuca and Robert C. Ramirez (directors), *Joseph: King of Dreams* (DreamWorks, 2000).

15. Genesis 40:18–19 (NIV).
16. Genesis 41:38–40 (NIV).
17. Acts 10:14 (author's translation).
18. Acts 10–11 (NIV).
19. James 1:5 (author's translation).
20. Donald Miller and Tetsunao Yamamori, *Global Pentecostalism: The New Face of Christian Social Engagement* (Berkeley: University of California Press, 2007), p. 60.

Chapter Eight: Hope, Joy, and Emotion

1. Donald Miller and Tetsunao Yamamori, *Global Pentecostalism: The New Face of Christian Social Engagement* (Berkeley: University of California Press, 2007), p. 17.
2. Oral Roberts, *Expect a Miracle: My Life and Ministry* (Nashville, Tenn.: Nelson, 1995).
3. Jeannette Cooperman, "Pentecostals Live with Hellfire and Joy," *National Catholic Reporter*, Nov. 12, 2004, pp. 1–2.
4. Stephanie Innes, "Hispanics Power City's Pentecostal Growth Spurt," *Arizona Daily Star*, Aug. 25, 2007, http://www.azstarnet.com/metro/198120
5. Ibid.
6. Converts to Pentecostalism from Catholicism outrank all other converts in most countries surveyed; the second-ranked previous affiliation of converts is in parentheses: Brazil, 45 percent (from no religion, 11 percent); Chile, 26 percent (from no religion, 11 percent); Guatemala, 35 percent (from no religion, 13 percent); Kenya, 20 percent (from Protestantism, 12 percent); Nigeria, 18 percent (from other religion, 13 percent); Philippines, 66 percent (from other religion, 6 percent).
7. Fernanda Santos, "A Populist Threat Confronts the Catholic Church," *New York Times*, Apr. 20, 2008, p. 30.
8. Innes, "Hispanics."
9. Ibid.
10. Chip Heath and Dan Heath, *Made to Stick: Why Some Ideas Survive and Others Die* (New York: Random House, 2007), p. 168.

11. Ibid., p. 166.
12. Ibid., p. 167.
13. Ibid.
14. Ibid., p. 203.
15. Pinnacle Peak Steakhouse, Nov. 14, 2008, http://www.pinnacle peaksteakhouse.com/noneckties.asp
16. Innes, "Hispanics."
17. Heath and Heath, *Made to Stick*, p. 167.
18. Miller and Yamamori, *Global Pentecostalism*, pp. 5–6.
19. Santos, "Populist Threat," p. 30.
20. Ibid.
21. Miller and Yamamori, *Global Pentecostalism*, p. 39.
22. Ibid., pp. 42–43. Countering racism, conflict transformation, and international cooperation are not listed by Miller and Yamamori, but Pentecostals who are working on these issues can be found at Pentecostals & Charismatics for Peace & Justice, http://www.pcpj.org
23. Barna Group, "New Study Shows Trends in Tithing and Donating," Apr. 14, 2008, http://www.barna.org/FlexPage.aspx?Page=BarnaUpdateNarrowPreview&BarnaUpdateID=296
24. Muscular Dystrophy Association, Nov. 14, 2008, http://www.mda.org/telethon
25. Heath and Heath, *Made to Stick*, p. 203.
26. Ephesians 2:12 (NIV).
27. Matthew 13:45–46 (author's translation).
28. Hebrews 11:33–35 (NIV).
29. John 4:14, 6:35 (NIV).
30. Pew Forum on Religion and Public Life, *Spirit and Power: A 10-Country Survey of Pentecostals* (Washington, D.C.: Pew Forum on Religion and Public Life, 2006), p. 24.
31. Titus 2:13 (NIV).
32. Romans 5:3–5 (author's translation). My mother actually quoted the King James Version: "Tribulation worketh patience; And patience, experience; and experience, hope: And hope maketh not ashamed; because the love of God is shed abroad in our hearts by the Holy Ghost."

33. Romans 12:12 (NIV).
34. Romans 15:13 (NIV).
35. Matthew 13:44 (NIV).
36. Psalms 28:7, 47:1, 66:1, 107:22, 126:3 (NIV).
37. Nehemiah 8:10 (NIV).
38. John 11:35; Matthew 26:75 (NIV).
39. Joel 1:13 (NIV).
40. Psalms 30:5 (AMP).
41. Cooperman, "Pentecostals."
42. Miller and Yamamori, *Global Pentecostalism*, p. 24.
43. Brian McLaren, "Reflections on Amahoro-Africa, May 2007," May 23, 2007, http://www.brianmclaren.net
44. Albert G. Miller, "Pentecostalism as a Social Movement: Beyond the Theory of Deprivation," *Journal of Pentecostal Theology*, Oct. 1996, pp. 97–114.
45. Harvey Cox, *Fire from Heaven: The Rise of Pentecostal Spirituality and the Reshaping of Religion in the 21st Century* (Boston: Addison-Wesley, 1995), p. 86.
46. Allan Anderson, *An Introduction to Pentecostalism: Global Charismatic Christianity* (Cambridge: University of Cambridge Press, 2004), p. 283.
47. Miller and Yamamori, *Global Pentecostalism*, p. 23.
48. Ibid., p. 49.
49. Ibid., p. 23.
50. Barbara H. Fiese, Thomas J. Tomcho, Michael Douglas, Kimberly Josephs, Scott Poltrock, and Tim Baker, "A Review of 50 Years of Research on Naturally Occurring Family Routines and Rituals: Cause for Celebration?" *Journal of Family Psychology*, 2002, 16, 381.
51. Miller and Yamamori, *Global Pentecostalism*, p. 23. See also Rebecca Pierce Bomann, *Faith in the Barrios: The Pentecostal Poor in Bogotá* (Boulder, Colo.: Rienner, 1999).
52. Miller and Yamamori, *Global Pentecostalism*, pp. 221–222 (emphasis mine).

THE AUTHOR

Paul Alexander is a fourth-generation Pentecostal from Kansas who became an atheist in his twenties while studying for a Ph.D. in religion. He slowly journeyed his way back to faith and now passionately promotes peacemaking and social justice with Pentecostals & Charismatics for Peace & Justice (an organization he cofounded in July 2001, which can be found on the Web at http://www.pcpj.org).

As a Pentecostal theologian and ethicist, Alexander has addressed audiences as large as six thousand; delivered a keynote speech in The Hague, Netherlands, on religions and human rights; and lectured and worked in Europe, India, Latin America, and the Middle East. He is the author of *Peace to War: Shifting Allegiances in the Assemblies of God*, editor of the *Pentecostals, Peacemaking, and Social Justice* series, and professor of theology and ethics and director of the Doctor of Ministry program at Azusa Pacific University in Azusa, California. Alexander and his family live in Southern California.

INDEX

Pentecost, 6, 49
Pentecost Rejected (Hill), 105
Pentecostal Place.com, 19
Peretti, F., 108–109
Peter: and emotion, 143; and healing miracles, 6; and rebuke of Simon, 106; and tongue-talking, 49, 50; visions of, 127–128
Pharoah, dreams of, 126
Philip, 106, 113
Pinnacle Peak Steakhouse, 136–137
Positive confession, 68–69, 73–74
Positive thinking, power of, 62–63
Potiphar, 81
Poverty, 70–78
Power encounters. *See* Spiritual warfare
The Power of Positive Thinking (Peale), 62
Praise songs, 36
Prayer: and prayer chains, 9; and praying with faith, 7–9; and suffering, 9–14; and tongue-talking, 50–54
The Prayer of Jabez (Wilkinson), 70–78
Presley, E., 35–36
Prophecy: and appeal of Pentecostalism, 129–130; in Bible, 125–128; and divine revelations, 118–125; problems with, 128–129
Prophetic dream ministry, 117–118
Prosperity gospel: in contemporary world, 63–67; and greed vs. economic insufficiency, 70–78; and Malachi 3:10-12, 64; origins of, 61–63; problems with, 67–70
Prostitution, in India, 148

Q

Qur'an, 16

R

Racism, 124–125
Ramírez, D., 33, 34
Rapture of the Church, 141

Rebekah, 81
Regina's story, 119–120
Rich Christians in an Age of Hunger (Sider), 63
Richardson, G., 68
A River Runs Through It (film), 46
Roberts, O., 1, 63, 132
Ruis, D., 31
Russell, V., 76–78

S

Samaritan woman, 140–141
Sample, T., 25–27, 28, 30, 31, 79
2 Samuel 6:1-22, 23
Sarah, 81
The Satan Seller (Warnke), 89
Satanism, 89
Saul. *See* Paul the Apostle
Save the Children, 134–137
"Seed faith," 61
Sempangi, K., 90
Sermon on the Mount, 73
Seymour, W., 37
Shamans, conversion of, 89–90
Sherwood, M., 117–118, 125
Shouting, 23, 36
Sider, R., 63
Simon, 106
Sister Marlena, 19–20
Smith, J.K.A., 55, 56
Social action, 138, 139, 148–149
South Korea, 101–102
Spirits. *See* Spiritual warfare
Spiritual focus, in Christianity, 73–74
Spiritual warfare: and appeal of Pentecostalism, 110–114; and Dawn's story, 95–96; definition of, 100–101; and "demon vision," 108–110; and Dr. Malek's story, 96–98; and exorcism stories in Bible, 102–107; and failure, 107–108; and healing miracles, 101–102; and Nadira's story, 98–99; and territorial spirits, 99–101